Beginning C++ Compilers

Berik I. Tuleuov • Ademi B. Ospanova

Beginning C++ Compilers

An Introductory Guide to Microsoft
C/C++ and MinGW Compilers

Apress®

Berik I. Tuleuov
Nur-Sultan, Akmolinskaia, Kazakhstan

Ademi B. Ospanova
Nur-Sultan, Kazakhstan

ISBN-13 (pbk): 978-1-4842-9562-5   ISBN-13 (electronic): 978-1-4842-9563-2
https://doi.org/10.1007/978-1-4842-9563-2

Managing Director, Apress Media LLC: Welmoed Spahr
Acquisitions Editor: Susan McDermott
Development Editor: James Markham
Coordinating Editor: Jessica Vakili

Berik dedicates the book to the memory of his father, Iglik K. Tuleuov. He expresses gratitude to his family for their endless patience while working on this book, colleagues and Apress editors for their kindness.

Contents

About the Authors

Berik I. Tuleuov is Senior Lecturer at L. N. Gumilyov Eurasian National University, Nur-Sultan, Kazakhstan. He's a researcher and mathematician using computers for scientific computations and designing algorithms. He runs a topic on The AIFC Tech Hub (a meeting point for global startups, entrepreneurs, investors, industry's top experts and talent pool) about Microsoft C/C++ compilers. This forum has more than two million registered participants. He regularly takes part in academic and industry conferences, mainly on computer science topics. Interests include programming languages, algorithms and data structures, concurrent (parallel) programming, scientific programming, (La)TeX Typesetting System, and data visualization.

Ademi B. Ospanova is an Associate Professor in the Department of Information Security at L. N. Gumilyev Eurasian National University. She is the author of many courses in the field of IT technologies. She is developer of educational programmes of all levels of the university on information security. In the educational process and projects she uses her own software and libraries in C/C++, C#, Java, Prolog, R, Python, Solidity, works in Mathematica, Maple, Sage packages. She also has her own website, including hosting on her own server.

She manages grant and initiative research projects, and her Masters and PhD students are winners of national scientific competitions.

She also gives courses and consultations on cryptography and programming to specialists from various companies.

About the Technical Reviewer

Sedat Akleylek received the B.Sc. degree in mathematics majored in computer science from Ege University, Izmir, Turkey, in 2004, and the M.Sc. and Ph.D. degrees in cryptography from Middle East Technical University, Ankara, Turkey, in 2008 and 2010, respectively. He was a Postdoctoral Researcher at the Cryptography and Computer Algebra Group, TU Darmstadt, Germany, between 2014 and 2015. He was an Associate Professor at the Department of Computer Engineering, Ondokuz Mayıs University, Samsun, Turkey, between 2016 and 2022. He has been Professor at the Department of Computer Engineering, Ondokuz Mayıs University, Samsun, Turkey, in 2022. He has started to work at the Chair of Security and Theoretical Computer Science, University of Tartu, Tartu, Estonia since 2022. His research interests include the areas of post-quantum cryptography, algorithms and complexity, architectures for computations in finite fields, applied cryptography for cyber security, malware analysis, IoT security, and avionics cyber security. He is a member of the Editorial Board of IEEE Access, Turkish Journal of Electrical Engineering and Computer Sciences, Peerj Computer Science, and International Journal of Information Security Science.

Acknowledgments

Ademi would like to dedicate the book to her fragile but strong mother who cares for her entire family. She provides Ademi with warmth and the opportunity to do her job.

Introduction

Anyone who wants to start programming in the C/C++ languages needs two things in general: a computer and two programs called a C/C++ language compiler and a source code editor (generally speaking, the so-called debugger — a program that helps find errors in the source code, but still it is not necessary). More, in principle, nothing is needed.

If any text editor (for example, Notepad on Windows) is in principle suitable as a source code editor, then the situation with compilers is not simple. On Windows, they must be installed, and in the vast majority of cases, when it comes to installing the C/C++ compiler, for some reason it means installing Microsoft Visual Studio, which requires a lot of computer resources. Meanwhile, Microsoft Visual Studio is not a compiler, but the so-called Integrated Development Environment (IDE), which includes, among other components, also a C/C++ language compiler.

As far as we know, there are no books devoted to installing C/C++ compilers[1], it is implicitly assumed that the user has the compiler either already installed, or its installation is standard and does not cause difficulties. However, there are many pitfalls here, and we will try to briefly describe the motives that prompted us to write our book.

Under Windows, usually installing a C/C++ compilers, especially Microsoft ones, takes quite a lot of time, because it comes with Microsoft Visual Studio for the vast majority of users. Installing Visual Studio requires usually about 40 GB of disk space and big amount of RAM, so it is impossible to use weak hardware. So we suggest an easy way to deploy Microsoft C/C++ compiler: no headache with disk space and hardware resources lack. Additionally, our means saves big amount of time since one can deploy software on removable devices, such as flash sticks, and use it easily in a portable way. We achieve this by using Enterprise Windows Driver Kit (EWDK), a single, large ISO file, which can be mounted as virtual device and used directly without any installation. EWDK contains everything from Visual Studio except IDE. EWDK also allows to use MASM64 (Microsoft Macro-Assembly) and C# compilers. With the aid of MSBuild System one can compile Visual Studio Projects (.vcxproj) and Solutions (.sln) even without Visual Studio! Analogously, MinGW compilers can be deployed from 7z/zip archives, simply by

---

[1] There are a lot of books on the C/C++ languages themselves.

unpacking into appropriate location. Briefly, both Microsoft C/C++ and MinGW compilers can be used as portable software. Notice that such approach does not require an administrative privileges at all.

It is Create Once, Use Many principle: one can deploy these compilers and auxiliary software on removable device and use everywhere, or just copy it to hard disk and use them from local disk. There is no need to re-install.

Also, users can use several versions of these compilers at the same time, they do not interfere each other. Using MSYS (Minimal SYStem, a port of GNU Autotools) allows to build under Windows many libraries originally designed for Unix-systems. These things important because standard installation procedure doesn't give such a flexibility: very often various versions of installed software conflict with each other, or it is impossible to install at all.

Our book is intended primarily for two categories of users:

• beginners to learn the C/C++ language, who don't want to spend time on the standard installation of MinGW and Microsoft C/C++ compilers, since in the first case one has to make a difficult and non-obvious choice between different builds of this compiler, and in the second — to solve computer resources lack and installation problems;
• advanced users who, generally speaking, are not professional programmers, but write small programs in standard C/C++, for, for example, scientific and technical calculations.

Of course, the approach we propose can also be useful for professional programmers, as it saves a lot of time; in addition, the created toolkit can be used in the future on a variety of computers without special preparation, since this toolkit is portable.

We describe the MinGW and Microsoft C/C++ compilers, the clang compiler is not covered (its popularity has not yet reached the level of first two). We set as our main goal the description of compilers, and not various IDEs, so they are practically not considered. Various advanced (lightweight) editors that have some IDE functions are considered as code editors. We do not consider the currently popular Visual Studio Code due to the fact that it is not lightweight (as we have already noted, the IDE is an auxiliary tool for us; however, if the user has enough memory installed on the computer, then nothing prevents using VS Code). We do not consider code debuggers, an interested reader can later deal with this topic himself.

Also, we do not consider WSL (Windows Subsystem for Linux), since this subsystem is designed to run Linux applications (and not all of them: for example, restrictions apply to GUI applications) under Windows, and we are fighting to build Open Source applications and libraries originally created for Unix systems for Windows. WSL, although it provides less resource consumption compared to virtualization, is still an additional layer that negatively affects the performance of applications running under it. The programs and libraries compiled under Windows using the tools we describe are native Windows applications and thus provide the highest performance.

For completeness of our research, we use a variety of versions of Windows, on different computers and virtual machines (GNOME Boxes, VMware). The system configurations on these platforms are different (different versions of Windows, different amounts of disk space, etc.), which explains why throughout the book the Programs, Soft, and User directories are located on various partitions of the computer's hard drive (and sometimes on removable devices). In part, we did this intentionally, because we wanted, in accordance with the spirit of our book, in every possible way to emphasize the flexibility and portability of the approach we use.

For the convenience of the reader, in the Appendixes we provide a number of tables to facilitate the use of the Microsoft C/C++ compiler. These tables are taken from the Microsoft website.

Files and Devices

1

General information on files and devices is given in this chapter. The concept of a file is fundamental to computer science, so it's important to be clear about it. The issues of effective user interaction with the computer are also discussed.

1.1   File Types and Formats

In general, a file is a piece of information with an assigned name that is stored on a computer media. The media could be a hard or SSD disk, compact or DVD disk, magnetic tape, flash sticks and cards, etc.

Most computers have at least one disk drive, HDD or SSD, installed permanently. Nowadays, laptops have no DVD drives at all. Almost all devices can be connected to a computer via USB; in this case, a user can use removable media: flash sticks and cards, external HDD/SSD disks, or CD/DVD media.

By type, computer files are divided into text and binary files. Text files contain bytes that have a visual representation, as well as bytes that serve to control (line feed, carriage return, tabulation). Simply put, the contents of a text file can be "read."

Microsoft Word files, although containing text information for the most part, are not text files, as they contain information about formatting, sizes and types of fonts used, and other meta-information, as well as other data, such as pictures. Generally, binary files can contain human-readable pieces too.

By format, files are divided into graphics, multimedia (video and audio), executables (programs), objects, archives, CD/DVD images, etc. On Windows, file formats are recognized by their so-called extension: three or more letters after the last period in the file name. For example, Adobe Acrobat Portable Document Format (PDF) files have the extension `'.pdf'`, and Microsoft Office documents have extensions `'.docx'`, `'.xlsx'`, etc. For many programs, file extensions are

© The Author(s), under exclusive license to APress Media, LLC,
part of Springer Nature 2024
B. I. Tuleuov, A. B. Ospanova, *Beginning C++ Compilers*,
https://doi.org/10.1007/978-1-4842-9563-2_1

not mandatory: for example, text editors can open the text file named "Readme"; however, some software require strong extensions for their files.

Most file formats are designed to be independent of processor platforms and operating systems. This means, for example, that the same pdf document can be opened on Windows, Linux, Mac OS, Android devices, and finally iOS. However, this is not the case for binary executables, which we will discuss as follows.

Note All files consist of bytes, both text and binary.

1.2   Executable and Batch Files

Before moving on, we need to make some clarifications. Most computer users, are dealing with a modern and convenient graphical shell that provides ease of work. The graphical shell of Windows is Explorer. The shell is an intermediary between the user and the operating system, allowing you to open files, run programs, etc. In the graphical shell, the mouse plays an important role, with which you can click the icons of programs and documents to launch and open them.

Note Mouse actions can be duplicated via the keyboard.

However, the graphical shell is not the only one—there is another one, which is called the command line. In the command line, the main role is played by another device—the keyboard. The command line is mainly used to run commands by typing the name of the command in the prompt and pressing the [Enter] key. The command can be either a system command (e.g., set or echo) or an executable program file, and you must specify the exact location (full path to this file) of this file. If such a file is not found due to nonexistence or an incorrect full path to it, the system will display a corresponding message:

```
E:\Test>mycommand
'mycommand' is not recognized as an internal or external command,
operable program or batch file.

E:\Test>
```

Commands can have parameters called options. Their number depends on the purpose of the command. As a rule, commands have built-in help, which in Windows is called like this:

```
E:\Test>echo /?
Displays messages, or turns command-echoing on or off.

  ECHO [ON | OFF]
  ECHO [message]
```

Type ECHO without parameters to display the current echo setting.

E:\Test>

Conventional notation [option] means that the 'option' parameter in square brackets [ ] can be omitted (and the brackets are omitted), and the ' | ' in ON | OFF means that one of the two options must be selected (sometimes, it happens that options can be combined, or, conversely, some options may be incompatible with some other options; such cases are specifically discussed in the help of the command).

For open source utilities, help is usually called in the format

E:\Test>command --help

So how to find this command line? Very simple: Press the [Win] + [R] keys and type cmd (cmd.exe is also possible) and press the [Enter] key. Windows will bring up a command prompt window.

Note In earlier Windows versions, this file was called COMMAND.COM. In modern Windows versions, this file is called CMD.EXE and is located in the C:\Windows\System32 directory.

Although the command line looks inconvenient, it undoubtedly has advantages over the graphical shell, especially when it comes to automating sequential actions, that is, for programming a certain sequence of operations. An example from the practice of one of the authors: It was required to extract all graphic files from a filled CD while maintaining the directory structure; there were many nested directories on the disk. In the graphical shell, this task is almost impossible to solve quickly, but on the command line, this task is solved in a couple of minutes, using the xcopy utility with the /s key (option).

Executable files contain program code that is executed by the central processor of a computer. Windows executable file formats include (by file extension) '.exe', '.com', '.dll', '.sys', '.ocx', etc.

- **exe**: The main format of Windows executable program files.
- **com**: This extension belonged a long time ago to 16-bit MS-DOS programs that were small and could use a small amount of RAM. On purely 32-bit and 64-bit operating systems, such programs cannot run (they can only run in compatibility mode or in emulators). Currently, Microsoft has made a change where the format of binary executable files is determined not by the extension but by the content of the file, so that any '.exe' file can be renamed to a '.com' file without breaking functionality. This change was made for compatibility with older MS-DOS batch files that called older utilities with '.com' extensions, the newer versions of which are already larger than the limits of the old '.com' format. Here is a list of these util-

ities: `chcp.com`, `diskcomp.com`, `diskcopy.com`, `format.com`, `mode.com`, `more.com`, and `tree.com`.

- **dll**: Dynamic-link libraries; they can contain both reusable executable code and data. The vast majority of Windows code reside in such libraries.
- **sys**: Windows device drivers; these files are binaries, and they are created by compilers from their human-readable source code in high-level programming languages such as C/C++ and Assembly (parts of drivers).

Windows `'.exe'` files have so-called "magic bytes": their first two bytes are always `'MZ'`.

Batch files on Windows have extensions `'.bat'` and `'.cmd'`.

Executable files in `'.exe'` and `'.com'` formats as well as batch files (`'.bat'`, `'.cmd'`) can be directly launched by the user. This can be done both in the graphical shell and on the command line. In the graphical shell, open the Explorer window, find the file to be launched, and double-click it. For the second method, launch the command prompt, type the full file name, and press the Enter key.

Notice that for binary executable files and batch files, when they are executed, their extensions can be omitted on the command line. In this regard, an interesting question arises: If the files `test.bat`, `test.cmd`, `test.com`, and `test.exe` are in the same directory, then which one will be executed when the `test` command is executed?

Answer: The order of execution is `'.com'`, `'.exe'`, `'.bat'`, `'.cmd'`; hence, `test.com` will be executed. To execute any other of them, you need to write its name in full with the extension, for example, `test.exe`. In general, the execution priority is determined by the `PATHEXT` environment variable and can be changed, which we will talk about later.

A batch file is a text file, each line of which consists of a single command that can have parameters. Thus, a batch file can execute several commands sequentially one after another, that is, by running one command, we actually execute a whole series of commands! Therefore, such files are sometimes called script files.

It is important to note that binary executables are not only operating system dependent but also processor architecture dependent: for example, Windows `'.exe'` files do not run on Linux or Mac OS; moreover, `'.exe'` files created for 64-bit Windows do not work in 32-bit Windows (the opposite is true: 32-bit Windows `'.exe'` files work in 64-bit Windows in compatibility mode). Likewise, Linux binaries don't work on Windows.

Batch files are a bit more flexible in this regard: while Windows `'.bat'` and `'.cmd'` files don't work on Linux, you can create script files on Windows that are cross-platform with some limitations. We will cover this in later chapters.

Note In Unix systems, every file can be made executable in terms of those systems.

1.3   System Commands

System commands are for executing common basic system commands. System commands are divided into internal and external ones. Internal commands are implemented in the CMD.EXE file; external commands are implemented as separate utilities located in the C:\WINDOWS\System32 system directory. An example of an external command is the abovementioned xcopy (xcopy.exe), an advanced file and directory copying utility.

Help on these commands, as noted earlier, can be called with the /?.

We briefly describe here some useful commands:

cls   clears the console window (clear screen).
set   sets a value to an environment variable.
echo   echoes its argument value.
cd   changes the working directory (change directory).
dir   types the content of the current directory.
path   displays the value of the PATH environment variable.

echo %PATH% types the value of the PATH environment variable.

1.4   Mounting Devices

Sometimes, in Windows you have to change the letter of the CD/DVD drive or even the hard disk partition. This can be done through the Computer Management applet, which is invoked by right-clicking the Computer icon in the Desktop. Note that this requires administrator rights.

Much more interesting and useful is the subst command, which does not require administrator rights and allows you to mount a folder as a disk partition, assigning a given letter to this disk:

```
E:\Test>subst /?
Associates a path with a drive letter.

SUBST [drive1: [drive2:]path]
SUBST drive1: /D

  drive1:         Specifies a virtual drive to which you want to
  ↪   assign a path.
  [drive2:]path   Specifies a physical drive and path you want to
  ↪   assign
to a virtual drive.
  /D              Deletes a substituted (virtual) drive.

Type SUBST with no parameters to display a list of current
  ↪   virtual drives.

E:\Test>
```

For example, the command

```
E:\Test>subst X: E:\Test
```

will create disk X: in the system (if it, of course, did not exist) and mount all the contents of the E:\Test directory on this disk. We will use this command later when working with the Microsoft C/C++ compiler.

1.5   Virtual Devices

Some software is shipped in the ISO format. Examples are Linux distributions, Microsoft Enterprise Windows Driver Kit, and others. As we know, the ISO file is an image of CD/DVD media, and in the old days, the user had to burn this file to a blank CD/DVD disk and insert the disk into the drive. In our days, it is much more easier to handle such files— it suffices to use the so-called virtual devices. The user just creates such a device and mounts the ISO file on the device.

We work with DVD virtual devices. Virtual devices are created programmatically; no physical device is needed. Such devices can easily be created on Windows 7 with the aid of several software: DAEMON Tools Lite (www.daemon-tools. cc/products/dtLite), Alcohol 120% Free Edition (http://trial.alcohol-soft.com/en/downloadtrial.php, all Windows operating systems except 98/ME, for personal use only), etc. These tools require installation and system reboot.

In our opinion, the best program of this kind is WinCDEmu, an open source CD/DVD/BD emulator (https://wincdemu.sysprogs.org); this program has a portable version (https://wincdemu.sysprogs.org/portable/). Portable single executable file runs under all versions of Microsoft Windows (10/8.1/8/7/2008/Vista/2003/XP), on both x86 and x64 platforms. No system reboot is needed.

WinCDEmu is

- Free for any kind of use.
- Lite, about 670 KB only.
- Easy to use, just run the downloaded portable exe.

Of course, WinCDEmu requires administrator privilege to create virtual devices and mount ISO images.

On Windows 10 and up, no additional software of this kind is needed at all. Just right-click the ISO image on the Explorer window and select the "Mount" menu item. The system itself will create the device, assign it a letter, and mount the image there—no matter if the user has administrator privilege or not (no matter if the user has administrative rights or not).

1.6   Conclusion

In this chapter, we have tried to clearly describe the concept of a file, which is fundamental for computer sciences, to classify them according to various features and ways of using them. It is also important to understand what executable and batch files are and the order in which executable files are launched.

Since we actively use virtual disks in the book, we have given a description of programs and commands for creating them.

Software Installation

2

2.1   Overview of Installation Methods

Every software on the computer should be installed in a certain way, in a certain location on the user's hard disk. The vast majority of software under Windows is installed in the `'C:\Program Files'` (`'C:\Program Files (x86)'` for 32-bit programs) folder.

Usually, every software resides in its own, so-called home folder. The home folder may contain a folder named bin, which stands for binary, containing the main executable file of the software. When you click this executable in the Explorer window or click this program icon in the start menu, the operating system launches it.

There is one more way to launch a program: from the command line. This way is the most flexible (but not convenient for simple users) one, and further we will consider it in detail. For Windows, the most popular (and widely used) way is its standard one: users should just click the installation file to get started.

In the old days, an installation package contained archived components of software and driver files designed for the installation of this software on a user's computer. An installation package includes also a file called Setup or something like which launches installation process; this file might be of exe or bat type.

The Setup program does the following:

- Extracts the components of the software being installed form archive into a temporary folder (usually TEMP)
- Copies extracted files into the appropriate location in the user's computer
- Modifies the Windows system registry for some parameters
- Carries out system-wide and user-level changes for some parameters such as PATH
- Creates system menu items and icons and desktop shortcuts for quick launch

© The Author(s), under exclusive license to APress Media, LLC,
part of Springer Nature 2024
B. I. Tuleuov, A. B. Ospanova, *Beginning C++ Compilers*,
https://doi.org/10.1007/978-1-4842-9563-2_2

Of course, not every Setup program does have to carry out every step of this scenario.

Sometimes, on updating, some software requires removing (uninstalling) the old version in order to proceed. Uninstalling software usually is quite straightforward but sometimes may cause problems, especially in the case of big packages such as Visual Studio. Notice that very often some registry items related to software being uninstalled stay undeleted and may cause errors on reinstalling.

Note It is not a good practice to add the path to the executable file of the software being installed into the environment variable PATH.

2.2   Installation Packages (msi)

In recent years, an installation package consists of a single file of exe or msi type. An exe file is a self-extracting archive, and msi is an archive which can be handled by Windows installation service.

The advantage of this installation way is that the user is supposed to make a minimal effort on installation: just click the file to start the installation process.

Note This way requires administrative privileges in most circumstances. Simple users cannot install such kind of software.

2.3   Installing with Archives

The most recent trends should be pointed out about the subject: more and more software packages are distributed not only in the form of msi but also zip/7z archives. In our opinion, this method is one of the most flexible and has the following advantages:

- No (traditional) installation is needed.
- Does not require administrative privileges.
- The Windows system registry is not affected, so several versions of the same software can be used simultaneously.
- Can easily be removed (uninstalled)—the user just deletes the program's folder.
- Can easily be relocated—the user just moves the program to another place and makes minimal change in one driver file.
- Can easily be cloned to another place analogous to the previous item.
- Can easily work from removable devices.

This method is especially suitable for compilers since these kinds of software are designed to work in the command line. Recall that compilers themselves have no visual interface; they always work in the command line.

The most popular GCC C/C++ compiler also works under Windows operating systems, and its port to these systems is called MinGW (Minimalist GNU for Windows). MinGW can be downloaded as (in the form of) both source code and `zip/7z` (sometimes, as self-extracting exe) archive packages.

Warning It is a common mistake to consider Visual Studio as a compiler. Visual Studio is a so-called IDE (integrated development environment) which includes compilers, editors, debuggers and other related stuff.

2.4   Installing from Sources

Another installation way is installing from the source code of a software or library. This way is the most flexible but complicated one.

The vast majority of Linux software are distributed with source code, together with prebuilt binaries.

However, many libraries are provided only in source code (binaries may cause compatibility issues on Linux systems), because usually it is easy to build from sources. These libraries could also be built under Windows, with some additional efforts.

Source code is written in high-level programming languages and should be compiled using the compilers of these languages, so users have to have the corresponding compilers installed in their system. We will discuss these topics further.

2.5   Portable Installation

Software packages distributed in the form of `zip/7z` archives can be burned into a CD/DVD disk after extraction from the archive so that they can work directly from CD/DVD.

It is even easier to write such programs to flash media and run from there. These are examples of the so-called portable installation.

2.6   Best Software Installation Practices for Windows Systems

Now let's talk about one installation method. This way looks somewhat complicated for normal users since it takes some effort; however, it is done once, and the results can be used many times afterward. Of course, these are only recommendations, not strong rules, but they save time and effort in the future.

Our first recommendation is not to install software in system default locations, such as `C:\Program Files`, except some software which require reinstallation after Windows reinstallation, such as Microsoft Office, Microsoft Visual Studio, Adobe software, etc.

Here are the reasons for doing so:

- Such kind of software requires fresh installation after Windows crash and reinstallation.
- It cannot be installed without system administrator privileges.
- It cannot be copied or moved to another place without disruption.
- It cannot be copied or moved to removable media without disruption.

Moreover, we strongly do not recommend installing the software in question on drive C: disk at all. The user had better divide their HDD, creating a new partition, and put their software and data there. In modern Windows versions, it is done so easily—it takes just five minutes to create a new disk partition! In Windows 10, right-click *My Computer*, select *Manage*, and then choose *Disk Management* from the window that appears. Select the C: disk in the lower part and right-click it, then select Shrink (Figure 2-1).

Here are the reasons for doing so:

- System crash does not affect user software and data.
- Software is ready for use after Windows recovery.
- No system administrator privileges are needed.
- Software can be copied or moved to any place.
- Software can be placed to removable media and launched in a portable way in another computer.
- Several versions of the same software can be used simultaneously.

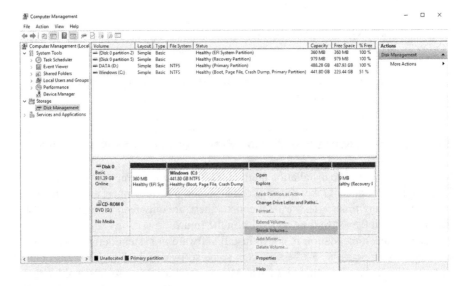

Figure 2-1 Creating a new partition

It is easy to launch the terminal window from any folder in the Linux graphical interface without the need to explore using the cd command. For a long time, this was not possible in Windows systems, but in the seventh version, such an opportunity appeared. The user just has to right-click a folder icon while holding the ⌈Shift⌋ button (Figure 2-1).

However, many users are missing the ' 'Open command window here' ' context menu item in the Explorer window in later Windows versions because Microsoft replaced it with a PowerShell launching item. PowerShell is too complicated for our purposes for many reasons; we will not discuss it here.

We strongly advise to do as follows. On the second disk partition, say D:, create the following folders: *Programs, Soft,* and *User.* These folders are to hold programs, software archives downloaded, and user data, respectively. Why do we store downloaded software in a place other than the default Downloads folder? The answer is this: usually, the Downloads folder is cluttered with a bunch of garbage, and it can be difficult to quickly find something there. In addition, in case of damage to the C: drive or reinstalling Windows, as we said earlier, this data will remain intact and can be reused. We will consider fine-tuning issues in the following chapters.

Sometimes, it is useful to change the drive letter assigned to a partition or CD/DVD device. How to do this using the same *Computer Management* snap-in is shown in Figure 2-2.

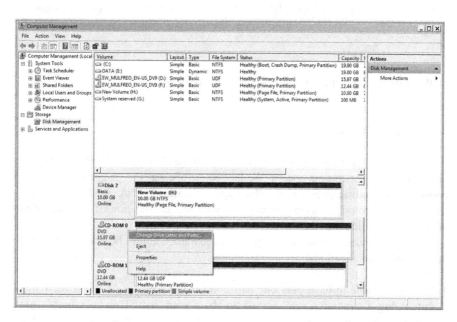

Figure 2-2 Changing the DVD letter

Let's describe in a generalized way our proposed method of installing some program under a conditional name, say, `SomeUtility-vX.Y.Z.7z`, where `X.Y.Z` means the version number of the program. Such programs, distributed as archives, have a `bin` subdirectory inside the archive, where the program's executable file (exe file) is located, as well as the dll dynamic libraries necessary for its operation (sometimes such libraries are not available). We must unpack the program archive into the `Programs\SomeUtility-X.Y.Z` directory. For the program to work correctly, the system needs to be told where the program's executable file is located, as well as the dynamic libraries necessary for its work—this can be done by adding the `Programs\SomeUtility-X.Y.Z\bin` directory to the PATH environment variable. To do this, we will create a batch file `SomeUtility-X.Y.Z.bat`:

```
@echo off

set PATH=%~d0\Programs\SomeUtility-X.Y.Z\bin;%PATH%
```

and place it in the `Programs\bin` directory, then add this directory to the system (if you have administrator access) or user PATH environment variable. How to do this is described in Section 6.2.1, page 58.

To use, we just invoke the command `SomeUtility-X.Y.Z[.bat]` from the command line. Of course, for convenience, you can name your batch file shorter, for example, `suXYZ.bat`, and then it can be invoked as `suXYZ`.

We demonstrate our approach with the help of a Figure 2-3.

2.7   Conclusion

In this chapter, we have given an overview of the methods for installing software on the Windows operating system. We looked at four ways to install software and considered the advantages and disadvantages of each of them. At the end of the chapter, our recommendations were given with the justification of our proposed method of installing the software.

In view of their importance, we repeat our recommendations here with somewhat more detailed justifications:

1. It is undesirable to have only one partition (disk) C: on your hard drive. When purchasing a computer, you can ask to share your disk. This operation is not difficult; you can do it yourself, with some experience, but it is better to ask a guru you know. In any case, it is better to do this when your disk is still slightly full, in which case the risks are minimal, and the process itself will take a little time.

```
D:
├─ Programs
│  ├─ bin
│  │  └─ 7zr.exe, mingw64.bat, msys.bat, msys2.bat, SomeProgram-X.Y.Z.bat,
│  │     vc.bat
│  ├─ EWDK_COMPACT
│  ├─ Far
│  ├─ Notepad++
│  ├─ mingw64
│  │  ├─ bin
│  │  │  └─ ar.exe, ld.exe,..., g++.exe, gcc.exe,...
│  │  └─ ...
│  ├─ MSYS
│  │  ├─ bin
│  │  │  └─ bash.exe, bzip2.exe, gzip.exe, lzma.exe, make.exe, tar.exe,...
│  │  └─ ...
│  ├─ ...
│  ├─ msys64
│  ├─ SomeProgram-X.Y.Z
│  │  ├─ bin
│  │  └─ ...
│  ├─ ...
│  └─ EWDK.iso
├─ Soft
│  ├─ msys+7za+wget+svn+git+mercurial+cvs-rev13.7z
│  ├─ SomeProgram-vX.Y.Z.7z
│  ├─ ...
│  └─ x64-4.8.1-release-posix-seh-rev5.7z
└─ Users
   └─ John
      ├─ C++
      ├─ Asm
      └─ Python
```

Figure 2-3 Disk D directory tree

For the C: drive, in which the Windows system itself is located, it is enough to allocate, say, 100 GB of space; the freed space can be allotted to the D: drive, on which it is advisable to store data. The meaning of these actions is that if the operating system breaks down (which happens quite often for various reasons: viruses, illiterate user actions, etc.), your data will most likely remain intact and will not be affected after the next reinstallation of Windows (recall that often, when installing Windows, users completely format the C: drive, hoping to get rid of viruses in this way).

2. Do not store data on the desktop! Do not store them in the so-called standard folders like My Documents either—these folders are located by default in the system partition (drive C:), and, if you are not a guru, then with such a breakdown of Windows, when only the command line is available to you, you will not be able to copy them. The data in such folders can be encrypted for security purposes, which also adds to the problems in their recovery.

   These problems can be avoided by storing data in the D: partition. Even if you format the C: drive by mistake when reinstalling the system, your data will remain intact. As for security, the users themselves can encrypt their data on the D: drive.

   Of course, the desktop is the very first place that comes to hand when you need to quickly save something; however, as we have already shown, this is not the best place. On the desktop, you only need to create shortcuts to folders with data—the loss of shortcuts is not critical compared to the loss of data.

3. When creating directories (folders), avoid using national (and other non-English) letters, as well as spaces! Until now, there are programs that incorrectly process such paths. At best, such programs will crash, and at worst, they will behave unpredictably, and the user risks wasting time looking for an unknown error.

   Spaces in directory names are also undesirable because when working in command-line mode, such paths have to be enclosed in (usually) double quotes, which is very inconvenient. For this reason, do not install, for example, compilers in the Program Files directory.

4. You should prefer such programs that do not require standard installation. The reason is that they do not require installation, which saves time, and when reinstalling the system, they do not need to be reinstalled. It should be noted that such programs, as a rule, do not use the Windows system registry. Examples of such programs are the Far Manager file and archive manager (http://farmanager. com/), the popular VLC media player (www.videolan.org/vlc/), advanced text editor Notepad++ (http://notepad-plus-plus.org/), various builds of the MinGW compiler (porting the GCC compiler to Windows), and there are more and more of them. Such programs are distributed in the form of an archive (zip, 7z, and other formats); to install them, it is enough to unpack them into some directory. There are several ways to customize the application, which are described in the next sections

For programs that do not require installation, it is better to allocate a separate directory, for example, `D:\Programs`.

Programming Languages and Software

3

Currently, there are a large, if not huge, number of high-level languages; however, when it comes to scientific and engineering computing, the choice narrows sharply, literally to three (and in fact, to two) languages: C/C++ and good old Fortran.

3.1 Programming Languages

3.2 C/C++

The C language was created in the early 1970s by Dennis Ritchie of AT&T Bell Laboratories (Bell Labs) to write the Unix operating system. The C language has had a huge impact on the computer industry: operating systems are written almost entirely in this language, and many popular modern languages (C++, C#, Java, JavaScript, and Objective-C) have actually borrowed its syntax.

Due to the presence of pointers in C, it is possible to write almost assembler programs that are characterized by high execution speed. And at the same time, C is much easier to write for most programmers than Fortran. Therefore, many modern libraries for scientific and engineering calculations are already written in C, not in Fortran.

The C language is standardized. In 1989, ANSI X3.159-1989 (ANSI C or C89) was adopted. In 1990, the ANSI C standard was adopted, with a few modifications, by the International Organization for Standardization (ISO) as ISO/IEC 9899:1990. In 1999, the ISO 9899:1999 (C99) standard was adopted. In March 2000, it was adopted and adapted by ANSI. On December 8, 2011, the new ISO/IEC 9899:2011 (C11) standard was published.

The canonical reference for the C language is the book by Brian Kernighan and Dennis Ritchie *The C Programming Language* often cited as KR or K&R, originally published in 1978 (by the way, it was in this book that the authors introduced the

B. I. Tuleuov, A. B. Ospanova, *Beginning C++ Compilers*, https://doi.org/10.1007/978-1-4842-9563-2_3

tradition of writing as the first program in the target language a program that prints the greeting "hello, world", since then it has become an unwritten rule). The current state of the language can be read in Ben Clemens' book *21st Century C.*

The C++ language was also created at AT&T Bell Laboratories, but by another person—Bjarne Stroustrup, a Dane living and working in the United States. Its original goal was to expand the C language by adding elements of object-oriented programming there; for this reason, at first the new language was called C with classes. In 1983, the language was renamed to C++ because it had grown from being a simple extension of the C language—there were so many additions. But despite all the changes, C++ remains compatible with the C language, with rare exceptions.

An important part of the C/C++ languages is the so-called standard library: for example, C does not have a formatted output operator like `write`/`writeln` in Pascal, but the `printf` function, which is found in the standard library. To use this feature, you must include the corresponding header file. Similarly, the C++ standard library includes not just input/output (I/O) classes and implementation functions and classes of this kind (e.g., `complex` for working with complex numbers) but also entire sublibraries of the STL type (STL, Standard Template Library, written by Alexander Stepanov and has long become part of the language), including sorting and searching algorithms. The language also provides work with strings and regular expressions, with various data structures (dynamic arrays, linked lists, binary trees, hash tables). In recent language implementations, classes for developing multithreaded and parallel programs have been added to the standard library, support for internationalization and classes for working with numbers (random numbers and distributions, numeric functions) have been improved. In addition, there are a huge number of utilities (e.g., clocks and timers).

Since 2012, C++ standards have been adopted on a three-year cycle. In 2020, the ISO/IEC 14882:2020 standard, often referred to as C++20, was adopted, which is the current one today. The C++23 standard is planned for this year (2023).

We recommend that you often look at https://cppreference.com, where you can get not only comprehensive reference information but also code examples illustrating the intricacies of using the element of the C++ language being studied. We also recommend a number of books ([4] to [10]) on scientific programming that use C and C++ to varying degrees.

The source code files of C programs have the `.c` extension, and the header files have the `.h` extension. C++ files use `.cpp` and `.cxx` extensions, while header files can have `.hpp` and `.hxx` extensions.

3.3   Fortran

Despite the seemingly solid old age (almost 60 years), the Fortran language is not going to give up its positions at all: in 2010, the next Fortran 2008 language standard was adopted, and work is actively underway on the next Fortran 2015 standard (a standard for programming languages alike, and for other areas, it is very important—e.g., the Delphi language was not standardized, and its Pascal prototype has already three standards and even more implementations that are incompatible between themselves; as a result, these languages are effectively dead). The Fortran language (FORmula TRANslator) was developed at IBM in 1957 by a group of specialists led by John Backus and was de facto the first high-level algorithmic language (the first was the Plankalkul language, in German—calculus plan, designed by the German engineer Konrad Zuse in 1945, but he did not have the opportunity to implement his language; implementation completed only in 2000).

The main advantage of Fortran is the presence in the source code of carefully written, debugged, very efficient, and well-documented software packages (libraries) for scientific and engineering calculations. A number of such libraries are available commercially: NAG Numerical Library from The Numerical Algorithms Group (NAG), IMSL Numerical Libraries (Rogue Wave Software), etc. These libraries enjoy well-deserved prestige among specialists.

Another advantage of the Fortran language is the high speed of code execution. In this parameter, Fortran is close to assembly language. Fortran is perhaps the most standardized language: FORTRAN IV (FORTRAN 66, 1972), FORTRAN 77 (1980), Fortran 90 (1991), Fortran 95 (1997), Fortran 2003 (ISO/IEC 1539-1:2004), Fortran 2008 (ISO/IEC 1539-1:2010). The language is actively developing; for example, the Fortran 90 standard introduced a free format for writing code, as well as elements of object-oriented programming, which were further developed in the Fortran 2003 standard (in fact, the list of innovations is huge: actually, this is like a new language; for those who studied the classical version of the language, the amount of changes can be assessed only by studying the new standard). In the latest versions of the standards, a lot of attention is paid to parallel computing.

3.4   Assembly

Assembly language allows you to create the shortest and fastest programs, but the price of this is the large size of the source code. From this point of view, the use of this language is inefficient, since it requires a lot of labor. However, this language has its own niche—where you need a small code size and high speed of its execution. Therefore, assembly code is used when writing drivers, as well as when writing some components of the operating system that closely interacts with the hardware, the so-called HAL (hardware abstraction layer).

One of the most common assemblers for Windows is the Microsoft Macro Assembler (MASM), which is part of the Microsoft C/C++ compiler. It must be emphasized that MASM is not supplied separately. We will briefly consider working with it in subsequent chapters.

Assembly source code files have the extension .asm.

3.5   C#

The C# object-oriented language was developed by Microsoft and is intended primarily for developing business applications. C# source code files have the extension .cs.

This language has a number of advantages that distinguish it from modern high-level languages; however, in our opinion, the presence of a couple of other shortcomings makes it completely unsuitable for use in the field of scientific and engineering calculations:

- C# is a platform-specific language, that is, only Windows applications can be written in it. Attempts were made to port the .NET Framework runtime to Linux (the Mono project), but this project did not gain much popularity for various reasons.
- Applications written in C# are actually executed on a virtual machine—for this reason, they are inferior in execution speed to C/C++ applications.
- Poor implementation of real types can lead to cumulative rounding errors! Because of its importance, we will address this issue in more detail.

Here are some extremely interesting quotes from Joseph Albahari and Ben Albahari's book *C# 5.0 in a Nutshell, Fifth Edition* [3]. They concern the use of the C# language in calculations. First, let's clarify some definitions of the basic types used in calculations. These are quotes from [3, page 24]:

> Of the *real* number types, float and double are called *floating-point types* and are typically used for scientific calculations. The decimal type is typically used for financial calculations, where base-10–accurate arithmetic and high precision are required.

and [3, page 29]:

> double is useful for scientific computations (such as computing spatial coordinates). decimal is useful for financial computations and values that are "man-made" rather than the result of real-world measurements.

Finally, we will quote in full from the short subsection *Real Number Rounding Errors* [3, page 30]:

> **Real Number Rounding Errors**
> float and double internally represent numbers in base 2. For this reason, only numbers expressible in base 2 are represented precisely. Practically, this means most literals with a fractional component (which are in base 10) will not be represented precisely. For example:

```
float tenth = 0.1f;                         // Not quite 0.1
float one = 1f;
Console.WriteLine (one - tenth * 10f); // -1.490116E-08
```

> This is why float and double are bad for financial calculations. In contrast, decimal works in base 10 and so can precisely represent numbers expressible in base 10

Figure 3-1 C# program

```
using System;

class Program{
  static void Main(){
    float tenth = 0.1f;
    float one = 1f;
    float res = one-tenth*10f;
    Console.WriteLine(res);
  }
}
```

Result: -1,490116E-08

(as well as its factors, base 2 and base 5). Since real literals are in base 10, `decimal` can precisely represent numbers such as 0.1. However, neither `double` nor `decimal` can precisely represent a fractional number whose base 10 representation is recurring:

```
decimal m = 1M / 6M;  // 0.1666666666666666666666666667M
double  d = 1.0 / 6.0; // 0.16666666666666666
```

This leads to accumulated rounding errors:

```
decimal notQuiteWholeM = m+m+m+m+m+m; //
↪   1.0000000000000000000000000002M
double notQuiteWholeD = d+d+d+d+d+d;   // 0.9999999999999999989
```

which breaks equality and comparison operations:

```
Console.WriteLine (notQuiteWholeM == 1M);  // False
Console.WriteLine (notQuiteWholeD < 1.0);  // True
```

As an illustration, we give the texts of the simplest programs in C#[1] and C++, `CSharp.cs` and `CPP.cpp`, which implement a simple algorithm: the difference

$$1.0 - 0.1 * 10$$

is calculated and then the result is displayed on the screen (Figures 3-1 and 3-2).

Note that the rather strange result of this C# program was tested in Windows 7, for the .NET Framework versions 2.0, 3.5 and 4.0. There is no such error in Windows 10.

---

[1] In order to compile a program in C#, it is not necessary to install Microsoft Visual Studio; almost every Windows includes the .NET Framework, which contains the C# language compiler. To build, you need to run the command `C:\Windows\Microsoft.NET\Framework\v3.5\csc.exe CSharp.cs`

Figure 3-2 C++ program

```
#include <iostream>

int main(){
    float tenth = 0.1;
    float one = 1;
    float res = one-tenth*10;
    std::cout << res;

    return 0;
}
```

Result: 0

3.6   Conclusion

In this chapter, we have given a brief overview of the C/C++ and Fortran languages and also provided important information about the C# language regarding computational aspects.

We also mentioned assembly language in the Microsoft implementation—Microsoft Macro Assembler (MASM).

General Build Information

4

This chapter describes the process of building software on Unix-like and Windows systems. A way to port the build process on Unix systems to the Windows platform is given. New build tools in Windows are also given.

4.1   Unix Systems

The traditional tool for building programs and libraries in the world of Unix-like systems is the famous make utility. Depending on what the utility is "ordered" to do, it can do many things: compile files, create object files from them, build a library from them, or, by linking them with runtime libraries, create an executable file and place them in the specified directories in the system.

For all these purposes, the make utility calls the appropriate programs: the compiler is called to compile, the archiver is called to create archived libraries, and the linker is called for linking. make reads all these instructions from a special file called Makefile.

Makefile is a text file of a special format; for simple projects, it can be created manually; for large projects, there are automated tools creating such files.

Note The Makefile must reside in the root directory of the project.

Generally, Makefile contains a set of rules; a rule looks like this:

```
<targets ...>:  <prerequisites ...>
        recipe
        ...
        ...
```

© The Author(s), under exclusive license to APress Media, LLC, part of Springer Nature 2024
B. I. Tuleuov, A. B. Ospanova, *Beginning C++ Compilers*, https://doi.org/10.1007/978-1-4842-9563-2_4

Sometimes, another terminology is used for the rules:

```
<targets ...>:   <dependencies ...>
        command
        ...
        ...
```

make is guided by the rule in order to build the target file from the source files of the project. A target is usually the name of executable or object files; it can also be the name of an action to carry out. Examples of the latter are 'all', 'clean', 'install', and 'uninstall'; they are called 'Phony Targets' and are marked by .PHONY in Makefile. Usual targets may depend on several files.

Note Failure to follow the Makefile format (often incorrect indentation at the beginning of a line in the description of targets) leads to an error in the make utility.

Many parameters contained in the Makefile require clarification when trying to build on a specific computer. For example, the system may not have installed (or the wrong version) a required library, a compiler higher than a certain version may be required, etc. To check all build options, a redistributable program or library includes a special script called Configure. This script is usually written in bash, but other languages can also be used, such as Perl.

As a result of the successful operation of the Configure script, a Makefile is generated that is intended specifically for this computer.

Although some programs and libraries are also supplied in compiled (binary) form, sometimes it is better to recompile them for a particular machine. The thing is that the Configure script allows you to take into account, for example, the parameters of the central processor and, in the case of a latest generation processor, activates its capabilities.

This note is especially relevant to the GMP library, which is designed to work with very large numbers.

4.1.1   GNU Autotools (GNU Build System)

The basic sequence of commands for building programs and libraries with some variations comes down to the following:

```
$ ./Configure
$ make
# make install
```

For some libraries (e.g., for GMP), the stage of checking the built result is desirable, which is made by the command

```
$ make check
```

This step may take a significant amount of time.

Once the project is built, one can delete the object files as they are no longer needed. For large projects with hundreds of files, this frees up a lot of disk space.

It may also be required when rebuilding the project after some changes in the source texts of some files. This can be done with the command

```
$ make clean
```

There is also a command for uninstalling the software already installed:

```
$ make uninstall
```

4.2   Windows Systems

4.2.1   nmake Utility

The nmake utility supplied with the Microsoft C/C++ compiler is an analog of the make utility and of course is not compatible with it. We give its parameters:

```
D:\Users\John>nmake /?

Microsoft (R) Program Maintenance Utility Version 14.31.31107.0
Copyright (C) Microsoft Corporation.  All rights reserved.

Usage:  NMAKE @commandfile
        NMAKE [options] [/f makefile] [/x stderrfile] [macrodefs]
        ↪  [targets]

Options:

/A Build all evaluated targets
/B Build if time stamps are equal
/C Suppress output messages
/D Display build information
/E Override env-var macros
/ERRORREPORT:{NONE|PROMPT|QUEUE|SEND} Report errors to Microsoft
/G Display !include filenames
/HELP Display brief usage message
/I Ignore exit codes from commands
/K Build unrelated targets on error
/N Display commands but do not execute
/NOLOGO Suppress copyright message
/P Display NMAKE information
/Q Check time stamps but do not build
/R Ignore predefined rules/macros
/S Suppress executed-commands display
/T Change time stamps but do not build
```

```
/U Dump inline files
/Y Disable batch-mode
/? Display brief usage message

D:\Users\John>
```

4.2.2 Visual Studio .vcxproj and .sln Files

When developing modern software, especially large software, the so-called integrated development environments (IDEs) are used, which include not only high-level language compilers but also debuggers to facilitate finding errors in programs and optimizing their work, as well as advanced source code editors with syntax highlighting and auto-completion functions and an advanced hint system, a system for working with source code repositories and version control, a designer for designing a graphical interface. Some environments contain database tools.

Of course, the source code of such applications consists of many files, and they are usually combined into so-called Projects. The source code of such Projects consists not only of files in some high-level programming language but also of resource files (icons, images, audio and video, etc.) and settings files—up to the cursor position in a specific file opened in the source code editor. Projects are created in the IDE (of course, very simple Projects can be created by hand, following the appropriate file formats, but this is usually not necessary), and each IDE has its own format. Typically, IDE project files are XML files (text files with Unicode support).

Microsoft Visual Studio project files have the .vcxproj extension (for older versions of Visual Studio, .vcproj). Visual Studio projects can be grouped into so-called Solutions, which consist of multiple .vcxproj projects. It is interesting to note that Solutions can combine projects written in different programming languages. Solutions files have the extension .sln.

To build Visual Studio projects and solutions, MSBuild is a utility that is tightly integrated into Visual Studio and is currently its native build system. However, we note that it is not necessary to use MSBuild from the Visual Studio environment to build projects and solutions—MSBuild can be run from the command line too.

Undoubtedly, projects make life easier when developing complex programs, especially those with a visual interface. However, in practice, especially in academic and scientific environments, you have to write programs that consist of a single file (or a small number of files), and creating a project for such programs does not make much sense. It is also important to emphasize that projects are generally not cross-platform—they cannot be ported to another platform or operating system. For researchers (and not only for them), this situation is not acceptable: for example, having written an implementation of some algorithm in the standard C++ language, the author wants to test the program on different platforms and operating systems.

For the preceding reasons, the ability of development environments to compile individual files is important. As far as we know, in recent years, the developers of Microsoft Visual Studio have also paid attention to this.

4.2.3   MSBuild Build System

In the Microsoft paper "Walkthrough: Using MSBuild to Create a Visual C++
Project" [13], the process of MSBuild usage in the command line to build a Visual
Studio C++ project is demonstrated.

This article walks you through creating a `.vcxproj` project file for a console
C++ application. Along the way, some explanations are given about the structure
of the `.vcxproj` and `.props` files, as well as the variables (wildcards) used in
such files.

We don't recommend going deep into the structure of these files, because these
files are usually generated automatically by Visual Studio, and these XML files are
quite large, although not difficult to understand (in XML files, it's very easy to get
confused about the start and end tags). You should also be careful when manually
editing such files—due to a slightest mistake, the project or solution will not open
in Visual Studio or will not build at all.

To build the simplest "Hello, from MSBuild!" application, you do not need to
create a project at all, but on the other hand, we want to show the clumsiness of
projects with this simple example.

So create your source code file, `main.cpp`:

```
// main.cpp : the application source code.
#include <iostream>
#include "main.h"

int main(){
  std::cout << "Hello, from MSBuild!\n";
  return 0;
}
```

and auxiliary `main.h` header file—additional header files can be included in this
file:

```
// main.h: the application header code.
/* Additional source code to include. */
```

Now let's create a file of our project called `MyProject.vcxproj` in a text
editor. Recall that a project file is an XML file consisting of elements, which in turn
can contain child elements. The root element of a project is named `<Project>`,
and this element will contain seven child elements. These child elements are

- Three grouping tags `<ItemGroup>`, the first of which defines the configuration of the project, and the other two contain the names of the files, source code,
  and header.
- Three `<Import>` import tags define the location of the Microsoft Visual C++
  settings files.
- Another grouping tag `<PropertyGroup>` sets project settings.

1. Create a root element with a `<Project>` tag. We will insert child elements between a pair of opening `<Project>` and closing `</Project>` tags:

```
<Project DefaultTargets="Build" ToolsVersion="16.0"
  ↪  xmlns="http://schemas.microsoft.com/developer/msbuild/2003">
</Project>
```

Note the value of the `ToolsVersion` parameter: "14.0," "15.0," "16.0," and finally "17.0" mean Visual Studio 2015, Visual Studio 2017, Visual Studio 2019, and Visual Studio 2022, respectively.

2. Next, let's add a child `<ItemGroup>` element, which, in turn, contains two of its own `<ProjectConfiguration>` child elements that are similar to each other. As you can see, the `<ItemGroup>` tag is used to group subelements, while the `<ProjectConfiguration>` elements are used to define *debug* and *release* configurations for a 32-bit Windows:

```
<ItemGroup>
  <ProjectConfiguration Include="Debug|Win32">
    <Configuration>Debug</Configuration>
    <Platform>Win32</Platform>
  </ProjectConfiguration>
  <ProjectConfiguration Include="Release|Win32">
    <Configuration>Release</Configuration>
    <Platform>Win32</Platform>
  </ProjectConfiguration>
</ItemGroup>
```

3. Let's add an element of type `<Import>` that sets the default C++ project settings:

```
<Import Project="$(VCTargetsPath)\Microsoft.Cpp.default.props"
  ↪  />
```

4. Next, add a `<PropertyGroup>` grouping element with two subelements `<ConfigurationType>` and `<PlatformToolset>`.

   The `<PlatformToolset>` property value should be set to v140, v141, v142, and v143 for Visual Studio 2015, Visual Studio 2017, Visual Studio 2019, and Visual Studio 2022, respectively.

```
<PropertyGroup>
  <ConfigurationType>Application</ConfigurationType>
  <PlatformToolset>v142</PlatformToolset>
</PropertyGroup>
```

The full set of values for this parameter can be found in Table 9-5 in Section 9.2.5.

5. Add another element of type < Import > that sets the current C++ settings of the project:

```
<Import Project="$(VCTargetsPath)\Microsoft.Cpp.props" />
```

6. Insert a grouping < ItemGroup > element with two child < ClCompile > elements. They define a C/C++ source code and a header file:

```
<ItemGroup>
   <ClCompile Include="main.cpp" />
</ItemGroup>
<ItemGroup>
   <ClInclude Include="main.h" />
</ItemGroup>
```

< ClCompile > defines the build target, such targets are defined in special files.

7. And finally, we add another element of type < Import > that defines the target for this project:

```
<Import Project="$(VCTargetsPath)\Microsoft.Cpp.Targets" />
```

Now we have our project file completed:

```
<Project DefaultTargets="Build" ToolsVersion="16.0"
↪   xmlns="http://schemas.microsoft.com/developer/msbuild/2003">
  <ItemGroup>
    <ProjectConfiguration Include="Debug|Win32">
      <Configuration>Debug</Configuration>
      <Platform>Win32</Platform>
    </ProjectConfiguration>
    <ProjectConfiguration Include="Release|Win32">
      <Configuration>Release</Configuration>
      <Platform>Win32</Platform>
    </ProjectConfiguration>
  </ItemGroup>
  <Import Project="$(VCTargetsPath)\Microsoft.Cpp.default.props"
  ↪  />
  <PropertyGroup>
    <ConfigurationType>Application</ConfigurationType>
    <PlatformToolset>v142</PlatformToolset>
  </PropertyGroup>
  <Import Project="$(VCTargetsPath)\Microsoft.Cpp.props" />
  <ItemGroup>
    <ClCompile Include="main.cpp" />
  </ItemGroup>
  <ItemGroup>
    <ClInclude Include="main.h" />
  </ItemGroup>
  <Import Project="$(VCTargetsPath)\Microsoft.Cpp.Targets" />
</Project>
```

The project can be built by the command

```
MSBuild MyProject.vcxproj /p:Configuration=Release
```

MSBuild Build Targets In Microsoft's definition, *a build target is a named set of predefined or user-defined commands that can be executed during the build*. In solutions that include many projects, for example, you can specify a single project as a target, and then this particular project will be built. The clean target clears the build folder of the corresponding configuration (if Release, then the Release folder is cleared; if Debug, the Debug folder is cleared), that is, object and other auxiliary files are deleted, and a new log file is created. To set the build target, use the /t option:

```
MSBuild MyProject.vcxproj /t:clean
```

Note MSBuild has the following syntax: MSBuild.exe [options] [project file | directory] Note that options can be specified as follows: "-option", "/option" and "--option"

MSBuild Properties Some properties can be changed on the command line, such as Configuration and Platform. Configuration can be Debug or Release, and Platform can be, for example, Win32 or x64 (indicating the bitness of the operating system for Intel processors).[1] You can also change the PlatformToolset property on the command line. The project file we just created cannot be built using the Visual Studio 2022 build tools, so this setting can be changed on the command line by adding the /p:PlatformToolset=v143 option.

Here is the project build log:

```
G:\Users\MSBuild>MSBuild MyProject.vcxproj
  ↪ /p:Configuration=Release /p:PlatformToolset=v143


Microsoft (R) Build Engine version 17.1.0+ae57d105c for .NET
  ↪ Framework
Copyright (C) Microsoft Corporation. All rights reserved.

Build started 4/17/2023 5:18:53 PM.
Project "G:\Users\MSBuild\MyProject.vcxproj" on node 1 (default
  ↪ targets).
PrepareForBuild:
  Creating directory "Release\".
  Creating directory "Release\MyProject.tlog\".
InitializeBuildStatus:
  Creating "Release\MyProject.tlog\unsuccessfulbuild" because
  ↪ "AlwaysCreate" was specified.
ClCompile:
```

---

[1] There may be other platforms.

```
X:\Program Files\Microsoft Visual Studio\2022\BuildTools\VC\Toʃ
↪  ols\MSVC\14.31.31103\bin\HostX86\x86\CL.exe /c /Zi /nologo
↪  /W1 /WX- /diagnostics:column /O2 /Oy- /Gm- /EHsc /MD /GS
↪  /fp:precise /Zc:wchar_t /Zc:forScope /Zc:inline
↪  /Fo"Release\\" /Fd"Release\vc143.pdb" /external:W1 /Gd /TP
↪  /analyze- /FC /errorReport:queue main.cpp
   main.cpp
Link:
   X:\Program Files\Microsoft Visual Studio\2022\BuildTools\VC\Toʃ
↪  ols\MSVC\14.31.31103\bin\HostX86\x86\link.exe
↪  /ERRORREPORT:QUEUE
↪  /OUT:"G:\Users\MSBuild\Release\MyProject.exe" /NOLOGO
↪  kernel32.lib user32.lib gdi32.lib winspool.lib
↪  comdlg32.lib advapi32.lib shell32.lib ole32.lib
↪  oleaut32.lib uuid.lib odbc32.lib odbccp32.lib /MANIFEST
↪  /MANIFESTUAC:"level='asInvoker' uiAccess='false'"
↪  /manifest:embed /DEBUG:FULL
↪  /PDB:"G:\Users\MSBuild\Release\MyProject.pdb" /TLBID:1
↪  /DYNAMICBASE /NXCOMPAT
↪  /IMPLIB:"G:\Users\MSBuild\Release\MyProject.lib"
↪  /MACHINE:X86 /SAFESEH Release\main.obj
   MyProject.vcxproj -> G:\Users\MSBuild\Release\MyProject.exe
FinalizeBuildStatus:
   Deleting file "Release\MyProject.tlog\unsuccessfulbuild".
   Touching "Release\MyProject.tlog\MyProject.lastbuildstate".
Done Building Project "G:\Users\MSBuild\MyProject.vcxproj"
↪  (default targets).


Build succeeded.
    0 Warning(s)
    0 Error(s)

Time Elapsed 00:00:15.08

G:\Users\MSBuild>
```

To be able to build the project for 64-bit Windows, the project file must be supplemented with the appropriate group of parameters; they are highlighted in bold in the following listing:

```
<Project DefaultTargets="Build" ToolsVersion="16.0"
↪  xmlns="http://schemas.microsoft.com/developer/msbuild/2003">
  <ItemGroup>
    <ProjectConfiguration Include="Debug|Win32">
      <Configuration>Debug</Configuration>
      <Platform>Win32</Platform>
    </ProjectConfiguration>
    <ProjectConfiguration Include="Release|Win32">
      <Configuration>Release</Configuration>
      <Platform>Win32</Platform>
    </ProjectConfiguration>
    <ProjectConfiguration Include="Debug|x64">
      <Configuration>Debug</Configuration>
```

```
      <Platform>x64</Platform>
    </ProjectConfiguration>
    <ProjectConfiguration Include="Release|x64">
      <Configuration>Release</Configuration>
      <Platform>x64</Platform>
    </ProjectConfiguration>
  </ItemGroup>
  <Import Project="$(VCTargetsPath)\Microsoft.Cpp.default.props"
  ↪ />
  <PropertyGroup>
    <ConfigurationType>Application</ConfigurationType>
    <PlatformToolset>v142</PlatformToolset>
  </PropertyGroup>
  <Import Project="$(VCTargetsPath)\Microsoft.Cpp.props" />
  <ItemGroup>
    <ClCompile Include="main.cpp" />
  </ItemGroup>
  <ItemGroup>
    <ClInclude Include="main.h" />
  </ItemGroup>
  <Import Project="$(VCTargetsPath)\Microsoft.Cpp.Targets" />
</Project>
```

Here, we have given a simple example of using the MSBuild utility. For details on how to run this utility, see Section 9.2.5 (page 104), along with some of the other parameters of this utility.

4.3   Cygwin

To build under Windows software originally developed for Unix systems, you can also use the Cygwin platform, but we will not consider this option, since this approach does not meet the compactness and portability requirements that we adhere to. These issues are discussed in more detail in Section 8.1, page 75.

4.4   Cross-Platform Topics

The MinGW compilers discussed in this book, like the Microsoft C/C++ compiler, are cross-compilers, that is, they allow you to create code for different hardware or software platforms.[2] For example, with the help of GCC (remember that MinGW is a port of GCC to Windows), you can generate code from the Linux operating system that is designed to run on Windows.

---

[2] A hardware platform refers to the processor architecture for which it is intended the generated code, and under the program, the operating system on which this code is executed. Naturally, these two types of platforms can be combined.

The MinGW builds we offer allow you to create code designed for both 32-bit and 64-bit Windows, and both 32-bit and 64-bit versions of MinGW can do this. However, one must be careful not to mix libraries for different versions of Windows platforms; cross-platform issues are not included in our task, and we will not consider them.

Similarly, the Microsoft C/C++ compiler can create executable files for different processors and software platforms: `'x86'`, `'x86_amd64'`, `'amd64'`, `'x86_arm'`, `'x86_arm64'`, `Arm`, `Arm64`, `Arm64ec`, and `CHPE`.

In our book, we focus on the Intel x86_64 processor architecture, often also referred to as `'amd64'`, due to their greatest prevalence. 32-bit Windows is considered obsolete, but it can still be used, and our book can fully help with this. However, we prefer 64-bit Windows.

Also, note that the techniques for working with the Microsoft C/C++ compiler that we describe in our book can easily be applied in a similar way to non-Intel processor architectures.

4.5 Conclusion

In this chapter, we have given general information about the tools for building programs and libraries in different operating systems. The most important point is that Unix build tools have been mainly ported to Windows systems, which allows you to build libraries and programs under Windows that were originally developed for Unix systems.

Some Useful Open Source Utilities

5

This chapter discusses various free programs that improve the efficiency of advanced users, including a file manager, an advanced text editor, a universal archiver, a utility for working with msi packages, and a utility for mounting ISO images.

5.1   Far Manager

Far Manager is a free (shareware) utility. It can be downloaded from the website https://farmanager.com.

This program is a clone of the once famous program Norton Commander by Peter Norton and John Socha. It utilizes text mode to work, so it is very fast.

"Far" stands for "File and ARchive," so it is very convenient to work with files and archives. The program is highly customizable and allows the use of plug-ins. Users can view and edit text files in various encodings, including Unicode UTF-8; moreover, it is possible to convert between these encodings.

It is possible to view an arbitrary file in hexadecimal format. Very useful is the ability to search for files containing a given word.

Almost every type of archive can easily be unpacked with the aid of this program. For doing this, select the archive with arrow keys or the mouse and hit $\boxed{\text{Enter}}$, and select files to extract, then press $\boxed{\text{F5}}$. The selected content will be extracted to the place opened in the second panel.

B. I. Tuleuov, A. B. Ospanova, *Beginning C++ Compilers*, https://doi.org/10.1007/978-1-4842-9563-2_5

The program is especially useful when you need to select files with a specific extension in a directory with many files:

- Convenient display of the contents of directories on disks.
- Display a directory tree on a disk with the ability to navigate to the desired directory directly through this tree, and you can create, rename, and delete directories here.
- Easily create, edit, copy, rename, move, and delete files.
- Easy creation, renaming, and removal of directories. You can immediately create a directory with several levels of nesting, just like the mkdir/md `Folder\Subfolder1\Subfolder2\Subfolder3` command.
- View files of various formats: text, Word documents, graphic files, database files, and archives. Text documents can be viewed in hexadecimal format.
- Run commands through the built-in console, and the command history is preserved.
- Manipulations with attributes of files and directories.
- Search for files and directories by mask and timestamps, in subdirectories, which are case-sensitive.
- Search for files by incoming substrings in nested directories.

The interface consists of two panels. Each of the panels displays the contents of a directory, while these panels are independent in the sense that the users themselves can choose what to display there. In particular, it is possible to display the contents of the same directory in both panels. File and archive operations can be performed from one directory to another.

Each panel is a table that has a top header containing information about the current directory for that panel. The bottom lines of the table contain information about the selected object (file or directory): size, if it is a file, modification time, as well as information about the size of the current partition and free space. The rest of the panel space is used to list the names of directories and files in the current directory. Each directory or file occupies a separate line in the list; by default, the list is displayed in each panel in a two-column format (this format, of course, can be changed).

The ' .. ' characters at the beginning of the list mean the superdirectory, that is, the parent directory of the current directory. By pressing the `Enter` key on this line, you can go up one level.

Always one of the panels is active. In the active panel, one of the rows is highlighted in color, except for the case when the current one in the active panel is the root directory of a disk that does not contain any files. We will call such a selected line an active line, and such a line should not be confused with a file selected using the `Insert` key.

Also, information about the current directory of the active panel is displayed in the title of the Far window, and the command line at the bottom of the Far window switches to the current directory of the active panel.

5.1.1   Default Installation

The program can be downloaded from the official site (https://farmanager.com/download.php?l=en), under the Stable builds tag. Three types of builds are available: for portable installation as an archive, msi package for standard installation, and build for developers. The builds cover three Windows platforms—x86, x64, and ARM64—which correspond to 32-bit and 64-bit Windows and Windows for ARM-based devices, respectively. For a standard installation, you need to download the msi package through https://farmanager.com/files/Far30b6116.x64.20230311. msi and run it with administrator rights.

5.1.2   Easy Installation

For easy installation, download the archive from the official website (https://farmanager.com/download.php?l=en), selecting the archive button under the Stable builds tag. Unpack the downloaded archive using the 7z archiver to the `Programs\Far` directory.

The sequence of the unpacking process is shown in the figures (Figures 5-1, 5-2, and 5-3).

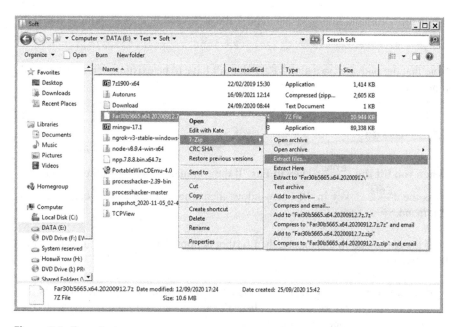

Figure 5-1   7z context menu

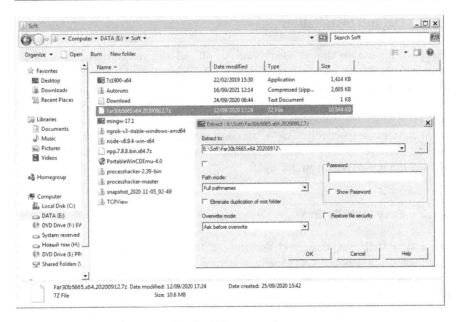

Figure 5-2 Hit the `..` button to select the folder to unpack

On the command line, you can unpack the archive with the following command:

```
7zr x -oD:\Programs\Far C:\Soft\Far30b6116.x64.20230311.7z
```

Note that the path `Programs\Far` doesn't have to be existing; it will be created if needed.

5.1.3   Usage

When you hit the `Enter` **key in Far** If the command line is not empty when you press the `Enter` key in the Far window, then what is there will be executed as a command.

If the command line is empty, then further actions depend on what is selected in the active line:

- If a directory name is selected, an entry will be made to that directory. If the name of this directory is `'..'`, then the current directory will be exited to the parent directory, one level higher.
- If an archive file name is selected (the file extensions are `'.zip'`, `'.7z'`, `'.rar'`, `'.tar'`, `'.gz'`, `'.tar.gz'`, `'.tar.xz'`, etc.), the table of contents of that archive file will be displayed. For files with double extensions

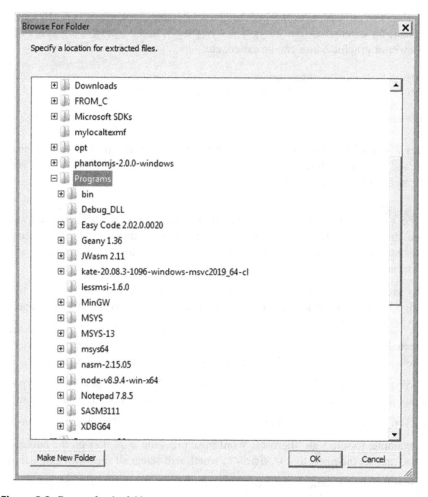

Figure 5-3 Browse for the folder

like '.tar.gz' and '.tar.xz', the internal archive file will be shown;
you can select it and press ⌐Enter⌐ again on its name to see the contents of the
nested archive. Having selected the entire contents of the archive with the hotkey
⌐Ctrl⌐ + ⌐*⌐ , you can unpack the archive with the ⌐F5⌐ key to the directory
displayed in the inactive panel.

- If a file name is selected whose extension is listed in the PATHEXT environment variable (these are '.com', '.exe', '.bat', '.cmd', '.vbs',
'.vbe', '.js', '.jse', '.wsf', '.wsh', and '.msc'), then the
operating system will execute this file. For other file name extensions, the
operating system will attempt to open the highlighted file using the application
associated with that extension: for '.txt', it is Notepad; for '.doc' and

'.docx', it is Microsoft Word; for '.xls' and '.xlsx', it is Microsoft Excel; for extensions like '.jpg', '.jpeg', and '.png', a graphic file viewer or graphic editor can be called; etc.

```
C:\Users\User>echo %PATHEXT%
.COM;.EXE;.BAT;.CMD;.VBS;.VBE;.JS;.JSE;.WSF;.WSH;.MSC

C:\Users\User>
```

Select files and directories Using Far, you can select a group of directories and files, and you can perform some operations on this group: copy, move, delete, and archive. Selected files are marked in yellow by default.

The Insert key is used to select a file or directory. Pressing this key again will cancel the selection. If the directory contains hundreds or thousands of files, then it makes no sense to select them individually. In this sense, the selection of files and directories by mask comes to the rescue.

By pressing * in the numeric keypad, you can select all files in the active panel, while directories are not selected. To select all directories and files at once, press Ctrl + * on the numeric keypad. If you press Ctrl + * on the numeric keypad when something is already selected, then the selection is inverted: the selected files become unselected, and the unselected ones become selected.

If you need to select by mask, you must press the + key in the numeric keypad and set the selection mask. If, among the selected ones, you need to cancel some, then you need to press in the numeric keypad - and set the appropriate mask. For example, to select all Microsoft Word files, press the + key on the numeric keypad and set the mask to '*.doc*', which will select all files with extensions '.doc' and '.docx', and press Enter. If now we want to exclude from the list of selected files all files whose name consists of five characters, then you need to press in the numeric keypad - and set the mask '?????.*', since this template will select all files whose name length is five (Figure 5-4).

Note We remind you that in the file name and extension, the symbol '*' means any number of any (allowed) characters, and '?' means any single (allowed) character or no character.

Selected files can be copied (F5), moved to another location or renamed (F6), deleted (F8), and archived (Shift + F1).

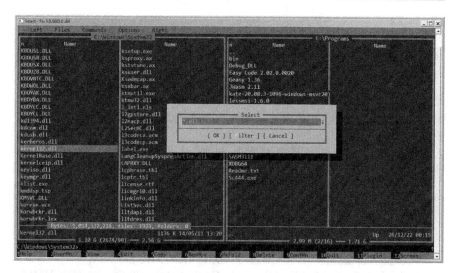

Figure 5-4 Selection by mask in Far

Figure 5-5 Quick find file in Far

Quick find file To do this, hit ⌊Alt⌋ + first file name letters. The search input form will appear at the bottom of the panel. The desired file or directory will be highlighted as soon as you enter enough letters to uniquely identify the file or directory you are looking for (Figure 5-5).

5.2   7z

7-Zip is a file archiver with a high compression ratio. The latest version is 7-Zip 22.01 (2022-07-15) for Windows.

7-Zip is free software with open source. Most of the code is under the GNU LGPL license. Some parts of the code are under the BSD 3-clause license. Also, there is unRAR license restriction for some parts of the code. Read 7-Zip License information.

You can use 7-Zip on any computer, including a computer in a commercial organization. You don't need to register or pay for 7-Zip.

The main features of 7-Zip according to the official website (www.7-zip.org) are

- High compression ratio in 7z format with LZMA and LZMA2 compression.
- Supported formats:
  - Packing/unpacking: 7z, XZ, BZIP2, GZIP, TAR, ZIP, and WIM
  - Unpacking only: APFS, AR, ARJ, CAB, CHM, CPIO, CramFS, DMG, EXT, FAT, GPT, HFS, IHEX, ISO, LZH, LZMA, MBR, MSI, NSIS, NTFS, QCOW2, RAR, RPM, SquashFS, UDF, UEFI, VDI, VHD, VHDX, VMDK, XAR, and Z
- For ZIP and GZIP formats, 7-Zip provides a compression ratio that is 2–10% better than the ratio provided by PKZip and WinZip.
- Strong AES-256 encryption in 7z and ZIP formats.
- Self-extracting capability for 7z format.
- Integration with Windows Shell.
- Powerful file manager.
- Powerful command-line version.
- Plug-in for Far Manager.
- Localizations for 87 languages.
- Works in Windows 10/8/7/Vista/XP/2019/2016/2012/2008/2003/2000.

p7zip is the port of the command-line version of 7-Zip to Linux/Posix.

On 7-Zip's SourceForge Page, you can find a forum, bug reports, and feature request systems.

5.2.1   Default Installation

For 64-bit Windows, the program can be downloaded from the official website (www.7-zip.org/download.html); there are choices between .exe, .msi, and .7z formats.

5.2.2 Easy Installation

`7zr.exe`, a 32-bit 7-Zip console executable, can be downloaded from the official website: www.7-zip.org/a/7zr.exe. As we recommended before, it is better to put this file into the `Programs\bin` folder to be always accessible in the command line.

5.2.3 Usage

```
C:\Users\User>7zr

7-Zip (r) 22.01 (x86) : Igor Pavlov : Public domain : 2022-07-15

Usage: 7zr <command> [<switches>...] <archive_name>
 ↪  [<file_names>...] [@listfile]

<Commands>
  a : Add files to archive
  b : Benchmark
  d : Delete files from archive
  e : Extract files from archive (without using directory names)
  h : Calculate hash values for files
  i : Show information about supported formats
  l : List contents of archive
  rn : Rename files in archive
  t : Test integrity of archive
  u : Update files to archive
  x : eXtract files with full paths

<Switches>
  -- : Stop switches and @listfile parsing
  -ai[r[-|0]]{@listfile|!wildcard} : Include archives
  -ax[r[-|0]]{@listfile|!wildcard} : eXclude archives
  -ao{a|s|t|u} : set Overwrite mode
  -an : disable archive_name field
  -bb[0-3] : set output log level
  -bd : disable progress indicator
  -bs{o|e|p}{0|1|2} : set output stream for output/error/progress
  ↪  line
  -bt : show execution time statistics
  -i[r[-|0]]{@listfile|!wildcard} : Include filenames
  -m{Parameters} : set compression Method
    -mmt[N] : set number of CPU threads
    -mx[N] : set compression level: -mx1 (fastest) ... -mx9
    ↪  (ultra)
  -o{Directory} : set Output directory
  -p{Password} : set Password
  -r[-|0] : Recurse subdirectories for name search
  -sa{a|e|s} : set Archive name mode
  -scc{UTF-8|WIN|DOS} : set charset for console input/output
```

```
-scs{UTF-8|UTF-16LE|UTF-16BE|WIN|DOS|{id}} : set charset for
↪  list files
-scrc[CRC32|CRC64|SHA1|SHA256|*] : set hash function for x, e,
↪  h commands
-sdel : delete files after compression
-seml[.] : send archive by email
-sfx[{name}] : Create SFX archive
-si[{name}] : read data from stdin
-slp : set Large Pages mode
-slt : show technical information for l (List) command
-snh : store hard links as links
-snl : store symbolic links as links
-sni : store NT security information
-sns[-] : store NTFS alternate streams
-so : write data to stdout
-spd : disable wildcard matching for file names
-spe : eliminate duplication of root folder for extract command
-spf : use fully qualified file paths
-ssc[-] : set sensitive case mode
-sse : stop archive creating, if it can't open some input file
-ssp : do not change Last Access Time of source files while
↪  archiving
-ssw : compress shared files
-stl : set archive timestamp from the most recently modified
↪  file
-stm{HexMask} : set CPU thread affinity mask (hexadecimal
↪  number)
-stx{Type} : exclude archive type
-t{Type} : Set type of archive
-u[-] [p#] [q#] [r#] [x#] [y#] [z#] [!newArchiveName] : Update options
-v{Size}[b|k|m|g] : Create volumes
-w[{path}] : assign Work directory. Empty path means a
↪  temporary directory
-x[r[-|0]]{@listfile|!wildcard} : eXclude filenames
-y : assume Yes on all queries

C:\Users\User>
```

5.3   Notepad++

Notepad++ is a free, open source multipurpose editor for Windows operating systems, so it is not cross-platform. Its official site is https://notepad-plus-plus.org.

Its key features are

- Multitab
- Syntax highlighting
- Column-mode edition: Ability to work with vertical text blocks (" ALT + mouse selection" or " Alt + Shift + Arrow key " to switch to column mode)
- Code folding

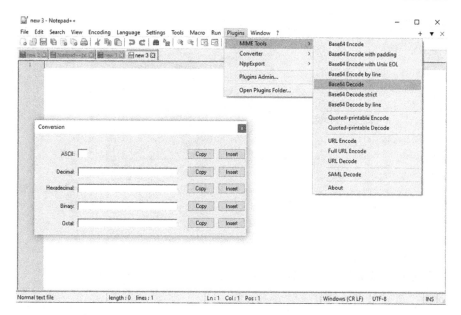

Figure 5-6 Notepad++ interface

- Auto-completion (text, parentheses, braces, and brackets)
- Support several text encodings and conversion between them
- Built-in MD5 and SHA256 hash calculation tools
- Bookmarks

Notepad++ supports almost all common programming languages, and the functionality of the editor can be extended using plug-ins (Figure 5-6).

A characteristic feature of the editor is that each group of operations is expanded in all sorts of ways. Let us discuss this in more detail. In the document, you can insert, for example, the current date in different formats. ASCII Codes Insertion Panel is shown in the picture (Figure 5-7).

One can copy to the clipboard Current Full File Path, Current File Name, Current Directory Path, All File Names, and All File Paths.

Eight options are given for case conversion, in particular, case inversion and randomizing. Of particular note are line operations: they can be cloned, delete duplicates, sorted, split, combined, moved up and down, insert/delete empty lines, reverse order of lines, rearrange lines randomly, and sort them according to different rules.

Windows, Linux, and Mac OS line endings are supported.

Users can trim leading and trailing spaces (simultaneously or not), convert EOL to space, and make conversion between [TAB] and [Space] in various

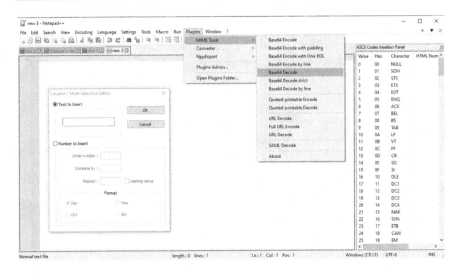

Figure 5-7 Notepad++ ASCII Codes Insertion Panel

combinations. These operations can be selected in the `Edit -> Blank` menu item. The file opened can be set to Read-only.

5.3.1   Default Installation

You should download it through https://github.com/notepad-plus-plus/notepad-plus-plus/releases/download/v8.4.9/npp.8.4.9.Installer.x64.exe for standard installation.

5.3.2   Easy Installation

Notepad++ suggests several options for easy installation; follow these links:

1. https://github.com/notepad-plus-plus/notepad-plus-plus/releases/download/v8.
   4.9/npp.8.4.9.portable.x64.zip
2. https://github.com/notepad-plus-plus/notepad-plus-plus/releases/download/v8.
   4.9/npp.8.4.9.portable.x64.7z
3. https://github.com/notepad-plus-plus/notepad-plus-plus/releases/download/v8.
   4.9/npp.8.4.9.portable.minimalist.x64.7z

Download the archive of your choice and extract it to the Programs directory. If necessary, you can make a shortcut for a quick launch on the desktop.

5.4 lessmsi

Its official site is https://lessmsi.activescott.com.

It is a small, wonderful open source utility to view and extract the contents of a Windows Installer (.msi) file. It was also called Less Msiérables as well as lessmsi. It can be useful when the user needs to work with a program that they cannot install due to lack of administrator rights.

Often, in such cases, it turns out that the program can actually be extracted from the msi installation package, and here this program comes to the user's aid.

This is a utility with a graphical user interface and a command-line interface that can be used to view and extract the contents of an MSI file.

5.4.1 Easy Installation

Download it through https://github.com/activescott/lessmsi/releases/download/v1.10.0/lessmsi-v1.10.0.zip. There is also a Chocolatey package available for installation.

Just unzip the archive into the `Programs\lessmsi-1.10.0` directory:

```
D:\Programs\lessmsi-1.10.0>dir
 Volume in drive D is DATA
 Volume Serial Number is 0ACA-8C17

 Directory of D:\Programs\lessmsi-1.10.0

03/14/2023  11:29 AM    <DIR>          .
03/14/2023  11:29 AM    <DIR>          ..
11/04/2021  03:24 AM             8,704
↪ AddWindowsExplorerShortcut.exe
10/10/2020  09:56 AM            19,968 LessIO.dll
11/04/2021  03:24 AM           105,984 lessmsi-gui.exe
11/04/2021  03:23 AM               172 lessmsi-gui.exe.config
11/04/2021  03:24 AM            25,600 lessmsi.core.dll
11/04/2021  03:24 AM            28,672 lessmsi.exe
11/04/2021  03:23 AM               176 lessmsi.exe.config
11/25/2018  02:07 PM            13,312 libmspackn.dll
11/25/2018  02:07 PM           167,936 mspack.dll
11/04/2021  03:23 AM         1,015,808 wix.dll
11/04/2021  03:23 AM           188,416 wixcab.dll
              11 File(s)      1,574,748 bytes
               2 Dir(s)  503,857,192,960 bytes free
```

5.4.2 Usage

To use it, after downloading the zip file, double-click `lessmsi.exe` to run the application.

You can also extract files from the command line. This has been used in automated scripts to extract files or information from an MSI. To extract from the command line:

```
lessmsi x <msiFileName> [<outouptDir>]
```

Here is an example of unpacking the msi package `VCForPython27.msi`; this is Visual C ++ 2009 for Python 2.7 from the official Microsoft website, required for Python 2.7. If you install this package in the standard way, then it will be installed somewhere in the wilds of the system user directories, and it will also not work correctly if the user account name contains Unicode characters, as well as spaces. Using `lessmsi`, this product can be simply unpacked and copied to the `Programs\VCForPython27` directory, while the package works without errors (Figure 5-8).

`lessmsi` can also integrate itself into Windows Explorer so that the user can right-click a Windows Installer file (`.msi` file) and select "Extract Files" to extract it into a folder right there. Shell integration can be dynamically enabled/disabled via a menu item Edit -> Preferences.

MSI Table Viewer Windows Installer files (`.msi` files) are based on an internal database of tables. lessmsi features a viewer for those tables. This is useful for people who work a lot with installers.

Figure 5-8 lessmsi

5.5   WinCDEmu

One of the best programs for mounting ISO images is WinCDEmu, which is an open source CD/DVD/BD emulator (https://wincdemu.sysprogs.org); this program has a portable version (https://wincdemu.sysprogs.org/portable). A portable single executable file runs under all versions of Microsoft Windows (10/8.1/8/7/2008/Vista/2003/XP), on both x86 and x64 platforms. No system reboot is needed. WinCDEmu is

- Free for any kind of use
- Lite, about 670 KB only
- Easy to use, just run the downloaded portable exe

5.5.1   Easy Installation

The download link for the portable version is https://github.com/sysprogs/WinCDEmu/releases/download/v4.1/PortableWinCDEmu-4.0.exe. Just put this single executable file in the folder `Programs\bin`.

5.5.2   Usage

Of course, WinCDEmu requires administrative privileges to create virtual devices and mount ISO images. On Windows 10 and up, no additional software of this kind is needed at all. Just right-click the ISO image on the Explorer window and select the "Mount" menu item. The system itself will create the device, assign it a letter, and mount the image there, no matter if the user has administrative privileges or not (no matter if the user has administrative rights or not).

However, some programs like UltraISO or WinRar may intercept a context menu item for ISO files and replace it with their own action, like "Extract." It is just the case when WinCDEmu comes to the rescue! In this case, just start WinCDEmu and select the ISO image you want to mount.

5.6   Conclusion

In this chapter, we have discussed several freeware programs that can be very useful.

These include a file and archive manager, a multifunctional (supporting many formats) archiving utility, a utility for unpacking standard Windows installation packages (msi), and a small program for mounting ISO images.

All of them, in addition, do not require traditional installation—they can be downloaded as archives, unpacked, and can start working. Moreover, they are quite small.

Command-Line Interface

6

More or less competent computer users who want to build their own libraries using compilers, as well as applications that use external libraries, should be able to work on the command line, understand the types of executable files, and know compilers well.

About compilers and related tools will be discussed later, but now we will give some basic concepts about the interfaces of the Windows operating system.

6.1 Command Interpreter

The command-line interface is traditionally thought to be native to Unix systems; however, this is not the case—the command line is invariably present in all versions of Windows. The reason is simple—with all the conveniences of a GUI, it has one important drawback: it is completely unsuitable for automation tasks, that is, for programming.

A funny and instructive incident happened to one of the authors many years ago: a user brought in a CD with a bunch of nested directories that, among other files, had graphic files that needed to be copied. This person did not know how to solve this problem in Windows, and manually browsing through all the directories, taking into account the nesting, was tedious and error-prone, as it can be easily confused. Meanwhile, the task was easily solved in a minute, even in Windows, with its heavily castrated command line in terms of functionality, using the command {xcopy} with the /s key.

Any computer can be considered as hardware + software; without software, we have only a pile of iron, and without iron, we have only programs on some medium. Both are useless on their own.

The most important program (or rather, a whole software package) that provides an interface between the hardware and the user is called the operating system. In

B. I. Tuleuov, A. B. Ospanova, *Beginning C++ Compilers*, https://doi.org/10.1007/978-1-4842-9563-2_6

other words, the operating system makes the hardware resources of the computer available to the user and provides for the installation of other, user programs, the so-called applications.

In turn, the program that provides the interface between the user and the operating system is called the shell of the operating system. There is a command-line interface (CLI) and a graphical user interface (GUI). The shell is used to execute operating system commands, for user interaction with the operating system.

Instead of the term command-line interface on Windows, it is usually called the command line or console, and on Unix systems, the terminal. We will also stick to these names.

The graphical shell of Windows is Explorer. It is important to note that, unlike Unix systems, the Windows GUI is hardwired into its kernel and cannot be unloaded. Unix systems can be used in a purely terminal mode, which is especially effective for web servers and scientific calculations—after all, in these cases, the graphic subsystem, which is gluttonous to memory and processor resources, is absolutely not needed! This explains, in particular, the fact that Linux operating systems are usually installed on supercomputers.

Let us note the main advantages and disadvantages of these shells. The main advantage of the graphical shell is the ease of operation; even a housewife can be relatively quickly taught to work more or less tolerably in Windows. The main disadvantage is that the graphical interface consumes too many computer resources (memory and processor time), which are especially necessary when solving scientific and engineering problems (a graphical shell is absolutely not needed to run and manage such tasks).

Another drawback of the graphical shell is a continuation of its main advantage—in an effort to simplify the life of the user, Windows Explorer does not allow, for example, the user to see what kind of file received by email they are going to launch (there are very common cases when, under the guise of a Word document or pictures, a Trojan virus is sent, just a file renamed accordingly) on their computer, because by default Windows Explorer does not display the file extension and does not have simple file content viewers, such as in Far Manager.

The main disadvantage of the command line for most users is the inconvenience of work—all commands have to be typed by hand. However, true professionals (hackers, administrators, developers, etc.) do not think so, since it is in this mode that the user has the greatest opportunities, and some tasks, in principle, cannot be effectively solved using the graphical shell.

The command line is also extremely effective at automating routine tasks.

The Windows command line can be invoked in several ways:

(a) Through the *Start menu | All programs | Command line*
(b) Through the *Start menu | Run*, then in the input window that appears, type cmd (recall that the executable file of the command interpreter is called cmd.exe and is located in the WINDOWS\system32 folder; in earlier versions, it was called command.com) and click OK.

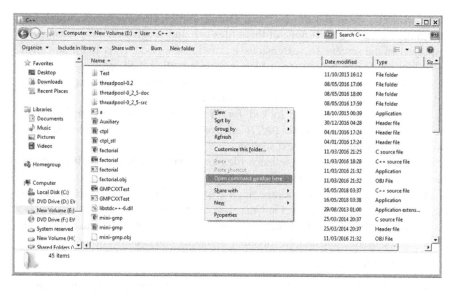

Figure 6-1 Opening the command line from Explorer

(c) By the key combination $\boxed{\text{Win}}$ + $\boxed{\text{R}}$, which is equivalent to selecting the *Start menu | Run*, then according to point (b).

Also, the command line can be launched from under the Explorer: while holding the $\boxed{\text{Shift}}$ key, just right-click the icon of the folder you want to open in the command line, or, while in this folder, do the same in an empty space, as shown in Figure 6-1.[1]

6.1.1 Launching and Executing Commands in the Command Line (Terminal, Console)

On Windows, typing at the command line (i.e., typing and pressing the Enter key) any sequence of characters that does not contain spaces will be treated as a command and will result in the execution of either an internal (e.g., as copy) command of the command interpreter or some program or batch file whose name matches the entered sequence; a command can be used with a parameter. If the user types, say, `dosmth` on the command line and presses $\boxed{\text{Enter}}$, then the shell looks for the `dosmth` internal command; if there is no such command, then it searches in turn for the

---

[1] This is true for Windows 7; on Windows 10/11, you will be prompted to run *PowerShell* instead of the command line. For these systems, this menu item can be reconfigured to launch a normal command line.

files dosmth.exe, dosmth.cmd, and dosmth.bat; if found, it launches such a file for execution. If none of these files is found, a corresponding message is displayed on the screen. The extensions *.cmd and *.bat refer to the so-called batch files (on Unix, these kinds of files are usually called shell scripts), sometimes called shell scripts; each line of such a text file consists of a command (possibly with parameters); these commands are executed one after another.

By default, these files are looked for in the current directory, and then in the directories specified in the PATH environment variable. We will talk about environment variables in the next section.

If the command or executable/batch file name contains spaces, then it should be enclosed in double quotes ("bad file name").

However, we strongly discourage the use of spaces in file and folder names, as well as non-English characters. On Unix, you can use single quotes.

On Windows, a file can be uniquely identified by giving its fully qualified name, including the drive name and the directory hierarchy that contains it, for example:

```
[drive:] [path] filename
```

According to accepted conventions, brackets [ ] denote optional elements, that is, they can be omitted.

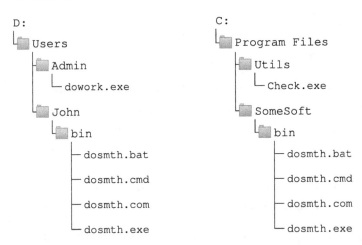

For example, the full file name of dosmth.exe for the preceding examples is

```
D:\Users\John\bin\dosmth.exe
C:\Program Files\SomeSoft\bin\dosmth.exe
```

To run these programs, you need to type the same lines on the command line, but in the second case, you need to enclose the line in double quotes due to the presence of spaces in the path:

```
C:\Users\John>"C:\Program Files\SomeSoft\bin\dosmth.exe"
```

Otherwise, the system will try to run the command or program named 'Program' located on the C: disk (C:\Program)—without finding which, it will display a corresponding warning, while the rest of the input string `'Files\SomeSoft\bin\dosmth.exe'` will be interpreted as the first parameter of the command being executed:

```
C:\Users\John>C:\Program Files\SomeSoft\bin\dosmth.exe
'C:\Program' is not recognized as an internal or external
    command,
operable program or batch file.
```

If the drive is not specified in the full file name, then the current drive is assumed, and if the path is not specified, then the current directory is assumed. Often, in the case when the full name of the file is indicated, one speaks of the *absolute* name of the file. But when the file name is specified relative to another directory, then they talk about the *relative* file name.

Let us explain the latter with examples. Let's say we are in the John directory, that is, the current directory is `D:\Users\John`. Then we can run our program by executing the command

```
C:\Users\John>bin\dosmth.exe
```

and to execute the program `D:\Users\Admin\dowork.exe`, while still in the John directory, we can type at the command line

```
C:\Users\John>..\Admin\dowork.exe
```

where `'..'` means the superdirectory, that is, the directory containing the current directory, in this case `D:\Users`. Less commonly (in Windows), the notation for the current directory is `'.'` (single dot). Both of these designations are widely used on Unix systems.

6.1.2 Path Separator

The Windows command interpreters command.com and cmd.exe understand both the default backslash (backward slash, backslash) `'\'` in file names and the forward slash (forward slash, slash) `'/'` (accepted in Unix systems). Although there are tips to use mostly forward slashes, this should be done carefully—because of the "curve" implementation of some commands and utilities by Microsoft programmers. For example, the dir command on the Windows 8 command line confuses forward slashes with switches: to avoid this, again, you need to enclose the paths in double quotes.

6.1.3 Windows Standard Command Line

The command line is the standard interface of the Windows command interpreter, cmd.exe.

Up until Windows 10, the command line was very inconvenient to use: the user could not even resize the window, for example. Now let's talk about some methods of setting up the command line.

For example, the standard prompt in the form of the current directory and the ' > ' sign can be changed with the command

```
C:\Users\John>set PROMPT=$D$_$$
```

to another format consisting of two lines: the first line displays the current date, and the second line shows the prompt in the form of the ' $ ' sign.

```
Mon 03/13/2023
$
```

The parameters of the PROMPT command can be found performing the PROMPT /?.

When forming a new invitation, you can use ordinary characters and special codes, the list of which is given as follows:

$A	& (Ampersand)	$L	< (less-than sign)
$B	| (pipe)	$N	Current drive
$C	((Left parenthesis)	$P	Current drive and path
$D	Current date	$Q	= (equal sign)
$E	Escape code (ASCII code 27)	$S	(space)
$F	) (Right parenthesis)	$T	Current time
$G	> (greater-than sign)	$V	Windows version number
$H	Backspace	$_	Carriage return and
	(erases previous character)		linefeed
		$$	$ (dollar sign)

One can also set the background and text colors using the COLOR command:

```
C:\Users\John>COLOR fa
```

This produces light green on bright white. Color codes are shown as follows:

```
0 = Black       8 = Gray
1 = Blue        9 = Light Blue
2 = Green       A = Light Green
3 = Aqua        B = Light Aqua
4 = Red         C = Light Red
5 = Purple      D = Light Purple
6 = Yellow      E = Light Yellow
7 = White       F = Bright White
```

For those users who display messages in national languages, it is useful to execute the command

```
C:\Users\John>chcp 65001
```

which sets the widely accepted UTF-8 variant of the Unicode encoding. In this case, the user should choose Consolas as the console font.

6.2   Environment Variables

Environment variables are used to store information that programs need to run. These are, for example, Windows installation and default application directories, processor type, etc. One of the important such parameters is PATH, which contains a list of directories in which programs called to be launched on the command line are searched, as well as dynamically loaded libraries necessary for the programs to run. The list of environment variables can be viewed with the set command. On a more or less clean machine, the result of this command looks like this:

```
C:\Users\John>set
ALLUSERSPROFILE=C:\ProgramData
APPDATA=C:\Users\John\AppData\Roaming
CommonProgramFiles=C:\Program Files\Common Files
CommonProgramFiles(x86)=C:\Program Files (x86)\Common Files
CommonProgramW6432=C:\Program Files\Common Files
COMPUTERNAME=COMPUTER
ComSpec=C:\Windows\system32\cmd.exe
DriverData=C:\Windows\System32\Drivers\DriverData
FPS_BROWSER_APP_PROFILE_STRING=Internet Explorer
FPS_BROWSER_USER_PROFILE_STRING=Default
HOMEDRIVE=C:
HOMEPATH=\Users\John
LOCALAPPDATA=C:\Users\John\AppData\Local
LOGONSERVER=\\COMPUTER
NUMBER_OF_PROCESSORS=8
OS=Windows_NT
Path=E:\Programs\bin;C:\Programs\bin;C:\Windows\system32;C:\Wind⌐
 ↪ ows;C:\Windows\System32\Wbem;C:\Windows\System32\WindowsPowe⌐
 ↪ rShell\v1.0\;C:\Windows\System32\OpenSSH\;C:\Users\John\AppD⌐
 ↪ ata\Local\Microsoft\WindowsApps;
PATHEXT=.COM;.EXE;.BAT;.CMD;.VBS;.VBE;.JS;.JSE;.WSF;.WSH;.MSC
PROCESSOR_ARCHITECTURE=AMD64
PROCESSOR_IDENTIFIER=Intel64 Family 6 Model 26 Stepping 5,
 ↪ GenuineIntel
PROCESSOR_LEVEL=6
PROCESSOR_REVISION=1a05
ProgramData=C:\ProgramData
ProgramFiles=C:\Program Files
ProgramFiles(x86)=C:\Program Files (x86)
ProgramW6432=C:\Program Files
PROMPT=$P$G
PSModulePath=C:\Program Files\WindowsPowerShell\Modules;C:\Windo⌐
 ↪ ws\system32\WindowsPowerShell\v1.0\Modules
PUBLIC=C:\Users\Public
SESSIONNAME=Console
SystemDrive=C:
SystemRoot=C:\Windows
TEMP=C:\Users\John\AppData\Local\Temp
TMP=C:\Users\John\AppData\Local\Temp
USERDOMAIN=COMPUTER
USERDOMAIN_ROAMINGPROFILE=COMPUTER
```

```
USERNAME=John
USERPROFILE=C:\Users\John
windir=C:\Windows
```

```
C:\Users\John>
```

Variables are given in the form VARIABLE=VALUE. As we can see from here, the PATHEXT variable sets the search order for executable files by their extensions, which was discussed earlier. This order can be changed if necessary using the command set.

Environment variables provide a convenient way to tell different programs about the presence of data or programs that they need to work on the system. For example, if the PYTHONHOME variable is set, the user program knows where the Python interpreter is located. To display the value of a variable, say PATH, you need to issue the command

```
C:\Users\John>echo %PATH%
```

The value of this variable is also displayed by the path command.

Environment variables can be modified, and there are two types of such changes: permanent and temporary. Permanent changes are made through the applet, are remembered, and will remain in effect even after the computer is restarted. Changes do not affect programs that were running before these changes and are applicable to newly launched programs. Sometimes, you need to restart your computer for these changes to take effect.

Temporary changes are made in the command line and are only effective for this console and expire after it is closed. Such changes are good because changes are made as needed, without clogging the system.

Environment variables are divided into system-wide and user variables. Administrator privileges are required to change system-wide variables.

6.2.1   Modification of the PATH System Environment Variable

It is inconvenient to write the full name of the file all the time (in fact, in Unix systems, the terminal remembers the entered commands, and on subsequent launches of the terminal, even after restarting the computer, a user can call them using the arrow keys; in Windows, Far Manager can do this), especially if it is long; therefore, the path to the directory where the user's executable file is located can be added to the PATH environment variable. Recall that this variable in text format contains a semicolon-separated list of directories in which to search for commands (executable files) and dynamic-link libraries.

The PATH variable can be modified by adding the user's path to it. This is done in several ways; usually, users do this: through the system applet (by pressing the Win + Pause/Break key combination, call up "System Properties," then edit "Environment Variables") or by editing the corresponding hive of the Windows

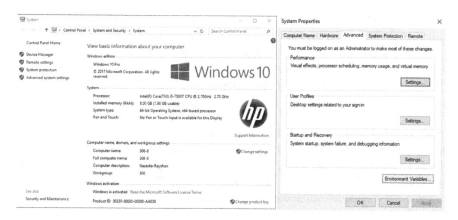

Figure 6-2 Modifying environment variables: System Properties

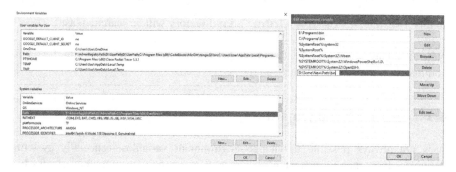

Figure 6-3 Modifying environment variables: PATH

registry; however, in this case, the system is clogged, since the changes made will remain, so to speak, forever (many programs, when installed, modify the PATH variable in this way; while uninstalling, they forget to clean up PATH).[2]

Now let's show the modification of environment variables in the graphical shell. You need to open the System window in the System settings, then click the Advanced system settings link; in the System Properties applet that opens, click the Environment Variables button again (Figure 6-2). After that, select the PATH variable at the bottom of the next window, under the inscription System variables, and click the Edit button. A new window will open called Edit environment variable (shown on the right side of Figure 6-3). To add a new directory, say D:\Some\New\Path\bin, to the PATH variable, click the New button and enter the string 'D:\Some\New\Path\bin' (you can also use the clipboard). To move this directory to the top of the list, use the Move Up button.

---

[2] One can often observe that the same path is present in the PATH list twice, in different places.

Changes will take effect for newly launched programs and consoles. Some settings (in particular, related to drivers) may require system restart.

More flexible, in our opinion, is another way, when the PATH variable is modified once, at the time of launch, so to speak, on demand. To do this, the user needs to give the following command on the command line:[3]

```
C:\Users\John>set PATH=D:\Users\John\bin;%PATH%
```

In this case, the PATH variable changes its value only for the current session; when the command line is closed, the changes are lost. By the way, we note that the Visual Studio command lines work exactly according to this principle. We also note that users can add their path to an arbitrary place in the PATH list; this only affects the search order—sometimes, there is a need to manipulate this. For example, one can write like this:

```
C:\Users\John>set PATH=%PATH%;D:\Users\John\bin
```

In this case, the D:\Users\John\bin directory will be searched last.

Note You can view the current value of the PATH variable by executing the path command on the command line.

6.3   Access Management

It is not always possible to change environment variables, especially system variables. In corporate environments, as well as on public computers, access to system settings can be severely restricted—changes can only be made by the system administrator. In such cases, a normal user may not even be allowed to change user environment variables, but if the user can run the command line, they can also change user variables like PATH from the command line using the set command.

The user can set up their own, user-defined environment variables, both system-wide (if they have administrator rights) and user-wide. This is done using the same set command:

```
set IS_VARIABLE_SET=YES
```

You can reset the value of a variable like this:

```
set IS_VARIABLE_SET=
```

---

[3] In a way, this is similar to the C++ assignment operator
$$PATH=D:\Users\John\bin + PATH$$
but for strings, because string addition is not permutable.

Make sure the variable name you choose, say VARIABLE_NAME, is not occupied (doesn't exist on the system). Otherwise, you can mess up its value. To check this, run the command

```
echo %VARIABLE_NAME%
```

If nothing is displayed on the screen, then the variable is free.

6.4   ConEmu

Official website: https://conemu.github.io
Download link:
www.fosshub.com/ConEmu.html?dwl=ConEmuPack.221218.7z
    Although the command line has improved in recent versions of Windows, we still recommend using a different, more advanced Windows console emulator. There are already many such emulators at the moment; there are very advanced ones, but with a commercial license. We suggest using open source ConEmu, which is free. The program is flexibly configured, and it is multitab; other console applications can be hosted in its windows, for example, Far Manager, cmd, PowerShell, or Unix PTY (cygwin, MSYS/MSYS2, WSL bash). For example, you can run ConEmu with several tabs at the same time, each of which runs different commands with different settings. To do this, you need to create the so-called startup file startup.txt (we will describe an example later) and run ConEmu with a command like

```
C:\Users\John>conemu.exe /cmd @startup.txt
```

We quote an example of such a file with comments from the official website of the program:

```
>E:\Source\FARUnicode\trunk\unicode_far\Debug.32.vc\far.exe
*/BufferHeight 400 cmd
/BufferHeight 1000 powershell
```

Each line in the file corresponds to a launched command. You may specify the console buffer height using the /BufferHeight parameter. If the line starts with ' > ', this tab will be active on startup. If the line starts with ' * ', this command will be run with administrator privileges (Figure 6-4).

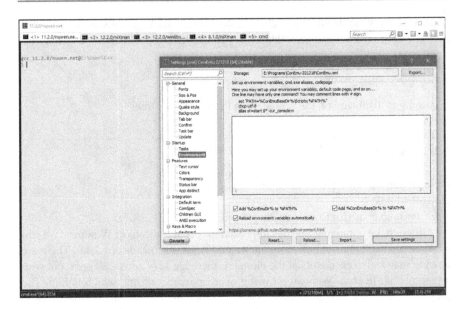

Figure 6-4 ConEmu with Settings open

6.5   Conclusion

This chapter is important for further understanding of the material presented in the book, since compilers and related utilities work on the command line. Therefore, we talked in some detail about the command line, environment variables, and how to modify them. At the end of the chapter, we talked about a convenient, multitab command-line emulator that allows flexible settings to suit the user's taste.

Integrated Development Environments and Editors

7

In this chapter, we describe some of the popular integrated development environments (IDEs) as well as lightweight advanced editors that provide some of the features of an IDE.

7.1   Microsoft Visual Studio

Currently, Microsoft Visual Studio is one of the most popular application development environments. The first versions of the product, when it was called Visual C++ and then Visual Studio, were very compact—Visual C++ 5.0 could be run directly from a CD; Visual C++ 6.0 also fit on one CD.

With all the advantages of this product, its exorbitantly increased volume is its main drawback. The disadvantages are also high demands on computer resources.

If a user has an insufficient powerful computer, then they cannot install Visual Studio, because it requires a large amount of disk space; also, the user cannot manage disk space distribution (Visual Studio will always require a large disk space on C:, as well as on any other disk).

Apart from disk space, Visual Studio needs a lot of RAM amount and good video support. Table 7-1 from the Microsoft site [14] shows hardware requirements for Visual Studio 2019. The Visual Studio 2022 Product Family [2] imposes slightly more requirements on video support.

For Visual Studio 2022, the requirements are about the same. In this case, we present only the hardware requirements.

Visual Studio 2022 Product Family System Requirements
Hardware

- 1.8 GHz or faster 64-bit processor; quad-core or better recommended. ARM processors are not supported.

© The Author(s), under exclusive license to APress Media, LLC,
part of Springer Nature 2024
B. I. Tuleuov, A. B. Ospanova, *Beginning C++ Compilers*,
https://doi.org/10.1007/978-1-4842-9563-2_7

Table 7-1 Visual Studio 2019 system requirements

Supported Operating Systems	Visual Studio 2019 will install and run on the following operating systems (64-bit recommended; ARM is not supported): • Windows 10 version 1703 or higher: Home, Professional, Education, and Enterprise (LTSC and S are not supported). • Windows Server 2019: Standard and Datacenter. • Windows Server 2016: Standard and Datacenter. • Windows 8.1 (with Update 2919355): Core, Professional, and Enterprise. • Windows Server 2012 R2 (with Update 2919355): Essentials, Standard, and Datacenter. • Windows 7 SP1 (with latest Windows Updates): Home Premium, Professional, Enterprise, and Ultimate.
Hardware	• 1.8 GHz or faster processor. Quad-core or better recommended. • 2 GB of RAM; 8 GB of RAM recommended (2.5 GB minimum if running on a virtual machine). • Hard disk space: Minimum of 800 MB up to 210 GB of available space, depending on features installed; typical installations require 20–50 GB of free space. • Hard disk speed: To improve performance, install Windows and Visual Studio on a solid-state drive (SSD). • Video card that supports a minimum display resolution of 720p (1280 by 720); Visual Studio will work best at a resolution of WXGA (1366 by 768) or higher.
Supported Languages	Visual Studio is available in English, Chinese (Simplified), Chinese (Traditional), Czech, French, German, Italian, Japanese, Korean, Polish, Portuguese (Brazil), Russian, Spanish, and Turkish. You can select the language of Visual Studio during installation. The Visual Studio Installer is available in the same 14 languages and will match the language of Windows, if available. **Note:** Visual Studio Team Foundation Server Office Integration 2019 is available in the ten languages supported by Visual Studio Team Foundation Server 2019.

(continued)

Table 7-1 (continued)

Additional Requirements and Guidance	
	• Administrator rights are required to install or update Visual Studio.
	• Refer to the Visual Studio Administrator Guide for additional considerations and guidance for how to install, deploy, update, and configure Visual Studio across an organization.
	• .NET Framework 4.5.2 or above is required to **install** Visual Studio. Visual Studio requires .NET Framework 4.7.2 to run, and this will be installed during setup.
	• .NET Core has specific Windows prerequisites for Windows 8.1 and earlier.
	• Windows 10 Enterprise LTSC edition, Windows 10 S, and Windows 10 Team Edition are not supported for development. You may use Visual Studio 2019 to build apps that run on Windows 10 LTSC, Windows 10 S, and Windows 10 Team Edition.
	• Internet Explorer 11 or Edge is required for Internet-related scenarios. Some features might not work unless these, or a later version, are installed.
	• The Server Core and Minimal Server Interface options are not supported when running Windows Server.
	• Visual Studio does not support application virtualization solutions, such as Microsoft App-V or MSIX for Windows, or third-party app virtualization technologies.
	• Running Visual Studio in a virtual machine environment requires a full Windows operating system. Visual Studio does not support multiple simultaneous users using the software on the same machine, including shared virtual desktop infrastructure machines or a pooled Windows Virtual Desktop host pool.
	• Running Visual Studio 2019 (Professional, Community, and Enterprise) in Windows containers is not supported.
	• For Hyper-V emulator support, a supported 64-bit operating system is required. A processor that supports Client Hyper-V and Second Level Address Translation (SLAT) is also required.
	• For Android emulator support, a supported processor and operating system are required.
	• Xamarin.Android requires a 64-bit edition of Windows and the 64-bit Java Development Kit (JDK).

(continued)

Table 7-1 (continued)

	• Universal Windows app development, including designing, editing, and debugging, requires Windows 10. Windows Server 2019, Windows Server 2016, and Windows Server 2012 R2 may be used to build Universal Windows apps from the command line.
	• Team Foundation Server 2019 Office Integration requires Office 2016, Office 2013, or Office 2010.
	• PowerShell 3.0 or higher is required on Windows 7 SP1 to install the Mobile Development with C++, JavaScript, or .NET workloads.

- Minimum of 4 GB of RAM. Many factors impact resources used; we recommend 16 GB of RAM for typical professional solutions.
- Windows 365: Minimum 2 vCPU and 8 GB of RAM. 4 vCPU and 16 GB of RAM recommended.
- Hard disk space: Minimum of 850 MB up to 210 GB of available space, depending on features installed; typical installations require 20–50 GB of free space. We recommend installing Windows and Visual Studio on a solid-state drive (SSD) to increase performance.
- Video card that supports a minimum display resolution of WXGA (1366 by 768); Visual Studio will work best at a resolution of 1920 by 1080 or higher.
  - Minimum resolution assumes zoom, DPI settings, and text scaling are set at 100%. If not set to 100%, minimum resolution should be scaled accordingly. For example, if you set the Windows display "Scale and layout" setting on your Surface Book, which has a 3000×2000 physical display, to 200%, then Visual Studio would see a logical screen resolution of 1500×1000, meeting the minimum 1366×768 requirement.

Visual Studio is a commercial product. For free use, there is Visual Studio Community Edition, which can be downloaded from the official Microsoft website.

Of course, this product has rich features, especially when working on large projects. However, for small projects, as well as for building libraries, it is quite possible to do without it; we will talk about this in the chapter on compilers.

7.2   Qt Creator

Official builds: https://download.qt.io/official_releases/qtcreator
Official mirror of the qt-project.org qt-creator/git repositories: https://github.com/qt-creator

Qt Creator is a cross-platform IDE designed primarily for C/C++ languages, but also supports Python, JavaScript, QML, and a number of others. Qt Creator is closely related to the cross-platform C++ library Qt.

Important information on Qt Creator, including compiling Qt Creator from sources for various platforms, is available at https://github.com/qt-creator/qt-creator.

Latest releases can be downloaded from the page: https://github.com/qt-creator/qt-creator/releases.

There are packages built with both MinGW and Microsoft C/C++ compilers: https://github.com/qt-creator/qt-creator/releases/download/v10.0.0/qtcreator-windows-x64-mingw-10.0.0.7z,

https://github.com/qt-creator/qt-creator/releases/download/v10.0.0/qtcreator-windows-x64-msvc-10.0.0.7z

```
qtcreator-windows-x64-mingw-10.0.0.7z   95.3 MB 2023-03-29
qtcreator-windows-x64-msvc-10.0.0.7z    90.6 MB 2023-03-29
```

We recommend downloading packages built with MinGW (Figure 7-1).

Qt Creator can automatically recognize the C/C++ compilers and versions of the Qt library installed on the system. However, you can easily connect any other compiler and, of course, the Microsoft C/C ++ compiler (in the figure, the abbreviation MSVC corresponds to this compiler; for compilers not listed in Figure 7-2, select the Custom menu item). For each compiler, you must specify the directory of that compiler's executable file, as well as a number of related options.

Figure 7-1 Qt Creator interface

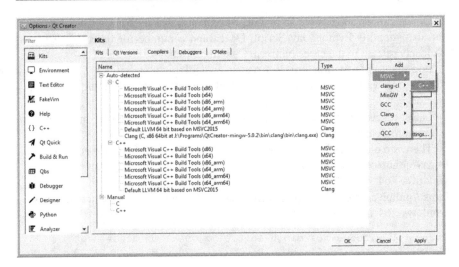

Figure 7-2 Qt Creator settings

7.3   Code::Blocks

Official website: www.codeblocks.org

Code::Blocks is a cross-platform, lightweight, free, and open source development environment (IDE) focused on the C/C++ and Fortran programming languages. It is very flexible and easily configurable. With the help of plug-ins, the functionality of Code::Blocks can be significantly extended. The list of supported compilers is very wide, and you can connect even those compilers that are not on the list.

Here is a quote from the official site:

> Built around a plugin framework, Code::Blocks can be extended with plugins. Any kind of functionality can be added by installing/coding a plugin. For instance, event compiling and debugging functionality is provided by plugins!

Other programming languages may be supported through the plug-in system.

Features such as syntax highlighting and code folding, C++ code completion, class browser, and a hex editor are naturally supported. It is important to note that although the environment is oriented toward C++ projects, it is easy to compile and build single-file programs without any configuration being required.

The IDE includes a complete debugger with rich functionality. It includes in particular

- Full breakpoint support
- Access to the local function symbol and argument display
- User-defined watches
- Call stack

- Disassembly
- Custom memory dump
- Thread switching
- CPU registers
- GNU Debugger Interface

Code::Blocks since version 13.12 includes a GUI designer called wxSmith. To fully develop applications based on the wxWidgets framework, of course, you need to install the wxWidgets SDK.

It is interesting to note that Code::Blocks can import Dev-C++ and Microsoft Visual C++ (MSVC 7 and 10) projects. Interaction with the GNU `make` and `qmake` projects of the Qt library is also provided through external `Makefiles`. The Code::Blocks projects themselves, like other IDE projects, use the XML format.

Binaries can be downloaded at www.codeblocks.org/downloads/binaries.

It is interesting to note that until recently Code::Blocks was distributed exclusively as an installable msi package, so administrator rights were required to install it. However, version 20.03 already offers different installation options, to quote the official site again:

The `codeblocks-20.03-setup.exe` file includes Code::Blocks with all plugins. The `codeblocks-20.03-setup-nonadmin.exe` file is provided for convenience to users that do not have administrator rights on their machine(s).

The `codeblocks-20.03mingw-setup.exe` file includes additionally the GCC/G++/GFortran compiler and GDB debugger from MinGW-W64 project (version 8.1.0, 32/64 bit, SEH).

The `codeblocks-20.03(mingw)-nosetup.zip` files are provided for convenience to users that are allergic against installers. However, it will not allow to select plugins/features to install (it includes everything) and not create any menu shortcuts. For the "installation" you are on your own.

More detailed information about binaries is given directly at the place where they are stored: https://sourceforge.net/projects/codeblocks/files/Binaries/20.03/Windows.

```
codeblocks-20.03mingw-nosetup.zip        2020-04-03     172.9 MB
codeblocks-20.03mingw-setup.exe          2020-04-03     152.4 MB
codeblocks-20.03-nosetup.zip             2020-04-03      37.2 MB
codeblocks-20.03-setup-nonadmin.exe      2020-04-03      37.5 MB
codeblocks-20.03-setup.exe               2020-04-03      37.5 MB
```

```
We offer different flavours of the Windows installer, explained
  hereby:

Installers:
- codeblocks-20.03-setup.exe
  -> Default installer WITHOUT compiler.
- codeblocks-20.03-setup-nonadmin.exe
  -> Default installer WITHOUT compiler but runnable as non-admin,
     too.
  (But will lack the ability to e.g. create shortcuts for all users
   etc...)
- codeblocks-20.03mingw-setup.exe
```

```
 -> Default installer WITH G++/GCC and GFortran compiler

Packages
- codeblocks-20.03-nosetup.zip
  -> Default package WITHOUT installer
  -> Same content as codeblocks-20.03-setup.exe after installation.
  (Allows no customisation, use "as-is" if allergic to installers...)
- codeblocks-20.03mingw-nosetup.zip
  -> Default package WITH G++/GCC and GFortran compiler but WITHOUT
     installer
  -> Same content as codeblocks-20.03mingw-setup.exe after
     installation.
  (Allows no customisation, use "as-is" if allergic to installers...)

32 bit Windows
- While we strongly recommend to install the 64 bit version, we also
  offer 32 bit versions esp. for older Windows versions.
- If needed, check the installers/archives in the sub-folder "32bit".
- If a compiler is included, we recommend also using the 32 bit
  compiler.
- Please respect that we provide only very limited support for these.

The installers/packages with compiler include the GNU compiler suite
and GNU debugger (GDB) from MinGW-W64 project (x86_64-posix-seh-rev0,
version 8.1.0).

Info to all installations:
-> To make Code::Blocks portable, create an empty
"default.conf" file in the installation directory!

IF UNSURE, USE "codeblocks-20.03mingw-setup.exe"!

Source: readme, updated 2020-12-29
```

Of course, we recommend to get `codeblocks-20.03(mingw)-nosetup.zip`. Just unpack it into `Programs\CodeBlocks-20.03`.

When Code::Blocks is first launched, it tries to automatically detect the compilers available on the system (Figure 7-3). As Figure 7-4 shows, the list of compilers supported by Code::Blocks is quite large.

The list includes Microsoft products that include the Microsoft C/C++ compiler, but the most recent of these is Microsoft Visual C++ 2010, which is long outdated and no longer supported. However, this does not mean that the latest Microsoft compilers cannot be used. In the following series of drawings, we will show an example of binding the Microsoft C/C ++ compiler from the EWDK package, which includes the compiler from Visual Studio 2019 (Figure 7-6).

First, you need to specify the path to the compiler executable file, `cl.exe`.

Next, you need to specify the `INCLUDE` and `LIB` directories in the EWDK directory tree.

Finally, let's demonstrate an example of a `Hello World` build and run (Figure 7-7).

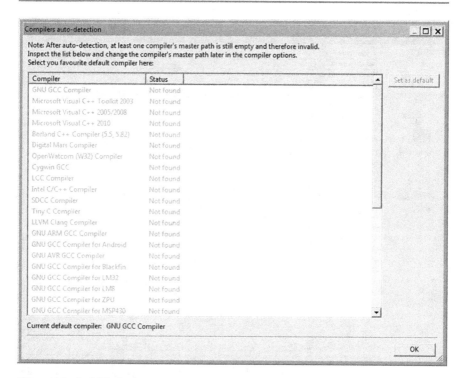

Figure 7-3 CodeBlocks first start

For the last EWDK package, which includes the compiler from Visual Studio 2022, you should replace the abovementioned folders with the next ones:

```
Program Files\Microsoft Visual
    Studio\2022\BuildTools\VC\Tools\MSVC\14.31.31103\include
Program Files\Windows Kits\10\Include\10.0.22621.0\ucrt
Program Files\Microsoft Visual
    Studio\2022\BuildTools\VC\Tools\MSVC\14.31.31103\lib\x64
Program Files\Windows Kits\10\Lib\10.0.22621.0\um\x64
Program Files\Windows Kits\10\Lib\10.0.22621.0\ucrt\x64
```

7.4   Geany

Geany official website: www.geany.org

As stated on its official website, Geany is a powerful, stable, and lightweight programmer's text editor that provides tons of useful features without bogging down your workflow. It runs on Linux, Windows, and MacOS, that is, cross-platform.

It can be downloaded from https://download.geany.org/geany-1.38_setup.exe. Unfortunately, portable builds do not yet exist for Geany. However, the installation file `geany-1.38_setup.exe` can be unpacked using 7z:

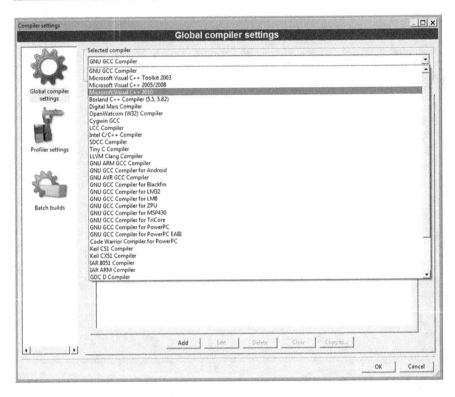

Figure 7-4 CodeBlocks compiler list

to do this, call the context menu in the Explorer window and select the
menu item 7z | Extract files.... After that, rename the unpacked
geany-1.38_setup directory to Geany-1.38 and move it to the
Programs directory.

```
cmd.exe /Q /C %c
```

7.5   Kate

Kate is a very convenient, multitab advanced text editor. The Unix version has a
built-in terminal; unfortunately, this feature is not implemented in the Windows
version, which somewhat reduces its attractiveness. It allows split screens both ver-
tically and horizontally. It also implements syntax highlighting for many languages
and code folding (Figure 7-8).

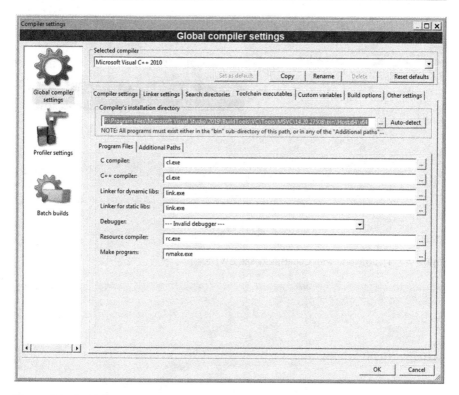

Figure 7-5   CodeBlocks: using a compiler from EWDK

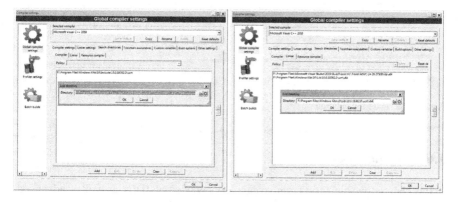

Figure 7-6   CodeBlocks Include and Lib directories from EWDK

Figure 7-7 Hello World with CodeBlocks and EWDK

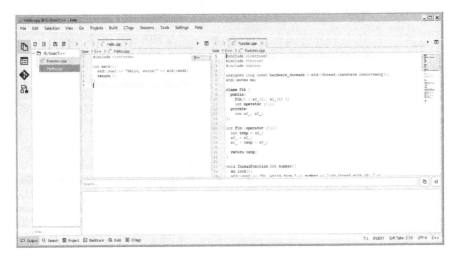

Figure 7-8 Kate for Windows

7.6   Conclusion

In this chapter, we have tried to give an overview of some IDEs, as well as advanced text editors that have some of the features of an IDE. Whenever possible, we chose free, cross-platform, and non-resource-intensive applications. This choice is justified by the fact that we mainly focus on users who deal with either small projects or applications consisting of a small number of files and mostly without the use of GUIs.

Minimal Systems

8

In this chapter, we will describe the MSYS and MSYS2 packages that allow many programs and libraries originally developed for Unix-like systems to be ported to Windows.

8.1 MSYS

MSYS stands for Minimal SYStem and is designed to provide a process for building under Windows programs and libraries that were originally oriented for building under Unix-like systems.

MSYS includes many GNU utilities such as `make`, `grep`, `gawk`, `gzip`, `tar`, `wget`, and the `bash` shell.

Warning: Naturally, we are not talking about full-fledged porting of these programs, since this is impossible for fundamental reasons.

MSYS doesn't include any compiler or C/C++ runtime libraries in it, it is part of the MinGW (Minimalist GNU for Windows) project.

MinGW provides free tools (utilities, WinAPI headers, and object libraries) and means (compilers, linker, and library archiver) for native Windows application and library development.

MinGW is based on the well-known Cygwin project (https://cygwin.com) developed by Red Hat. Cygwin is also intended to provide a means of porting programs and libraries from Unix-like systems to Windows, as well as a shell like `bash`; however, at the same time, it strives to ensure that the software being ported conforms to POSIX standards more fully. The implementation of such a goal requires an additional layer in the form of a shared library `cygwin1.dll`; in addition, Cygwin can only be used in programs distributed under the GNU GPL license. Also, making use of additional layer `dll` makes the programs created with Cygwin slow.

© The Author(s), under exclusive license to APress Media, LLC,
part of Springer Nature 2024
B. I. Tuleuov, A. B. Ospanova, *Beginning C++ Compilers*,
https://doi.org/10.1007/978-1-4842-9563-2_8

As for MSYS, there is no additional `dll` layer in it; WinAPI calls are used. Some Unix applications using the POSIX API (such as `fork`, `mmap`, or `ioctl`) compiled under Cygwin fail to build under MSYS.

Two versions of MSYS (often referred to as MSYS 1) and MSYS2 are currently supported, each with its own advantages and disadvantages.

MSYS

✓ Takes up little space.
✓ Very compact: The downloadable archive is only 45 MB in size.
✓ Self-contained: The `make` utility and other necessary programs are already included; nothing needs to be downloaded.
✓ Supports older versions of Windows.
✓ Easily portable.
✗ Does not support Unicode.
✗ Not frequently updated.
✗ 32-bit only.

MSYS2

✓ Has a package manager.
✓ More convenient console.
✓ Unicode support.
✗ Takes up a lot of space.
✗ Special file system requirements.
✗ Does not work on older versions of Windows.

Note MSYS can be used separately.

MinGW and MSYS provide an independent, highly portable (can be written to removable media) compact development environment that does not require installation.

8.2   Default Installation

For default installation, a user should go to the official website of the MinGW project. Currently, the MinGW project is moving from the old official site www.mingw.org to the new one located at https://osdn.net/projects/mingw.

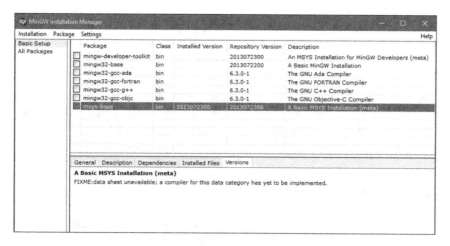

Figure 8-1 MSYS installation

The online installer `mingw-get-setup.exe` (can also be obtained from the new site) is still available at https://sourceforge.net/projects/mingw, in the files/Installer folder. Installation is quite straightforward: when you run this file, the necessary components are downloaded, then the MinGW Installation Manager (Figure 8-1) is launched in the window of which you can select the installation of MSYS. Note that as a result, the main utilities will be installed, a total of 152 files:

```
C:\MinGW\msys\1.0\bin>dir
 Volume in drive C has no label.
 Volume Serial Number is FAEC-928D

 Directory of C:\MinGW\msys\1.0\bin

02/19/2023  01:14 PM    <DIR>          .
02/19/2023  01:14 PM    <DIR>          ..
04/17/2010  06:53 AM           307,712 awk.exe
04/28/2010  09:14 AM            20,992 basename.exe
10/19/2014  11:27 PM           564,224 bash.exe
02/19/2023  01:14 PM             6,955 bashbug
. . .
04/17/2010  05:08 AM           109,568 grep.exe
04/17/2010  05:39 AM                65 gunzip
04/17/2010  05:39 AM             5,868 gzexe
04/17/2010  05:39 AM            64,512 gzip.exe
. . .
04/29/2010  09:18 PM           165,888 make.exe
04/18/2010  05:48 AM           245,760 makeinfo.exe
04/28/2010  09:14 AM            39,424 md5sum.exe
04/28/2010  09:13 AM            29,696 mkdir.exe
05/13/2010  04:13 AM             6,321 mount
07/13/2016  08:47 PM           821,248 msys-1.0.dll
. . .
```

```
04/17/2010   05:39 AM                  2,418 zmore
04/17/2010   05:39 AM                  4,954 znew
               152 File(s)     16,337,692 bytes
                 2 Dir(s)     812,740,608 bytes free
```

With this installation of MSYS, you can install MinGW in the same way, within the same process. At the same time, additional settings between these products are not required. However, in this case, the use of other versions of the MinGW compiler causes difficulties. Briefly speaking, this case of installation is not flexible.

8.3   Easy Installation

As we discussed in Chapter 2, easy installation means downloading the entire package as a single archive file and then unpacking it into the `Programs` directory. For MSYS, this will be the `Programs\msys` folder.

One of the places to get an all-in-one package of MSYS is the MinGW-w64 download page (http://sourceforge.net/projects/mingw-w64/files/Externalbinary packages(Win64hosted)/MSYS(32-bit)). The latest release is `MSYS-20111123.zip`, dated 2011-11-23, of size 51.0 MB.

A more recent build, supplemented with some useful utilities, can be downloaded from the MinGW-builds project page (http://sourceforge.net/projects/mingwbuilds/files/external-binary-packages). Here, one can find as the latest release a 45.1 MB file `msys+7za+wget+svn+git+mercurial+cvs-rev13.7z`, dated 2013-05-15.

The first archive contains (in the bin subdirectory) 398 files, while the second contains 545. We recommend taking the second archive which is also more fresh.

Although https://sourceforge.net/p/mingw-w64/wiki2/MSYS suggests to run `Programs\msys\msys.bat` and perform the command

```
sh /postinstall/pi.sh
```

there is no need in it. Just create a batch file named `msys1.bat` with the following content:

```
@echo off
call D:\Programs\msys\msys.bat
exit
```

and put it in the folder `Programs\bin`. Lazy readers can download it from the author's GitHub folder. Of course, disk letter change may be needed.

There is a trick that excludes the use of a drive letter. To do this, it is needed to change the preceding batch file like this:

```
@echo off
set HOME=C:\User\C++
call %~d0\Programs\msys\msys.bat
exit
```

Here, `set HOME=C:\User\C++` means that we set the home directory for
MSYS to `C:\User\C++`. The home directory can also be set as follows:

```
set HOME=/C/User/C++
```

We just write this path in MSYS syntax, with a slash path separator `'/'` instead of
a backslash `'\'` on Windows systems. Also, `'%~d0'` expands to the disk letter
where this batch file is located, so no disk letters are needed to handle.

8.4   Some Tips

On first launching MSYS bash, a file `.bash_history` will be created in the
MSYS home folder. As we mentioned earlier, this folder can be set in `msys.bat`.
The file `.bash_history` holds the history of all commands executed during
every bash session. One can list these commands with arrow keys, instead of
retyping them as in Windows (the Windows command line does not remember
previous session commands executed).

The `export` command, which is similar to the `set` command on the Windows
command line, will be very useful. The Windows command

```
set PATH=E:\Programs\mingw64-8.1.0\bin;%PATH%
```

in the MSYS system has the following analog:

```
export PATH=/E/Programs/mingw64-8.1.0/bin:$PATH
```

Windows drives `C:`, `D:`, etc., have `/c`, `/d`, etc., mount points in MSYS,
respectively. Pay attention to the path separator and the absence of a colon after
the drive letter.

8.5   MSYS2

The official website of the project is www.msys2.org. Unlike MSYS, MSYS2 is
available for 32-bit and 64-bit Windows and is updated quite often. There's also a
handy pacman package manager, but we don't recommend overusing it: packages
can quickly grow to 5 GB or more in total if a user is not careful. As stated on the
official website, its package repository contains almost 3000 prebuilt packages.

It should also be noted that MSYS2 has a very convenient terminal compared to
MSYS.

8.6   Default Installation

Standard installation of MSYS2 uses a big `exe`-archive which should be downloaded from the official website. The installer program requires 64-bit Windows 8.1
or higher (note that this is not the only artificial limitation; we will discuss them

later). For example, a user cannot install MSYS2 on Windows 7 (however, it is possible to use it on that system; we will consider this case in the next section).

Also, there is another restriction: no FAT volumes, only NTFS ones are allowed for the installation directory. The default installation folder is C:\msys64. Of course, administrator rights are required. In the rest, the setup process is pretty standard.

8.7   Easy Installation

Fortunately, there is another way of MSYS2 installation. With this method, a user can

✓ Work on older versions of Windows, in particular, under Windows 7
✓ Choose an installation folder even on FAT volumes

Also, no administrator privileges are required at all.

For this case, one should download archived package msys2-base-x86 _64-20230127.tar.xz. It can be downloaded from the following URL: https://repo.msys2.org/distrib/x86_64/. Note that there is also a slightly bigger self-extracting package msys2-base-x86_64-20230127.sfx.exe, but we do not recommend using it, as it will refuse to unpack correctly on non-NTFS partitions.

On the next step, we should extract archive content into the D:\Programs \msys64 directory; it is easy to fulfill with the aid of Far Manager. Finally, we create in the folder Programs\bin a batch file named msys2.bat of the following content:

```
@echo off
set HOME=C:\User\C++
%~d0\Programs\msys64\msys2.exe
exit
```

Note that msys2.exe automatically launches the bash interpreter.

On the first launch of MSYS2, we have

```
Folders:     1047
Files:       15759
Files size:  279 MB
```

in the installation folder. After initializing, a caution will appear which suggests restarting MSYS2 in order to apply necessary actions.

```
####################################################################
#                                                                  #
#                                                                  #
#                  C   A   U   T   I   O   N                       #
#                                                                  #
#                  This is first start of MSYS2.                   #
#         You MUST restart shell to apply necessary actions.       #
```

```
#                                                                        #
#                                                                        #
#########################################################################
```

As a result, several configuration files will be created:

```
Folders:     1054
Files:       15780
Files size: 279 MB
```

Unlike MSYS, there is no `make` utility in the base MSYS2 package, so we must install it:

```
$ make
-bash: make: command not found
```

It is done with the following command:

```
$ pacman -S make
```

This completes the MSYS2 installation process for our purposes.

8.8   CMake

CMake stands for cross-platform make and is designed to lighten software building, testing, and packaging processes. It is open source and consists, in fact, of tools family, as stated in its official website: https://cmake.org.

The main purpose of CMake is to generate, based on files called `CMakeLists.txt`, standard `Makefiles` for Unix systems, and for Windows—Visual Studio project/workspace/solution files.

Also, the Qt Creator and Visual Studio development environments natively support CMake.

Download: https://cmake.org/download/

Windows x64 Installer: `cmake-3.25.2-windows-x86_64.msi`

Windows x64 ZIP: `cmake-3.25.2-windows-x86_64.zip` ~40 MB, expands to 98 MB

8.9   Default Installation

The default installation is completely standard and easy: just run the `msi` file as an administrator and follow the instructions. As always, we recommend the installation from the archive file, which is completely simple, as usual, and does not require administrator rights.

8.10   Easy Installation

Just unpack the archive into `D:\Programs\cmake-3.25.2-x86_64`.
The utility has an implementation for both the graphical shell (`cmake-gui.exe`,
Figure 8-2) and the command line (`cmake.exe`), so it is easy to use it in batch
scripts, automating routine tasks.

```
Folders:    125
Files:      7090
Files size: 98.3 MB

Directory of D:\Programs\cmake-3.25.2-x86_64\bin

01/19/2023   09:26 PM    <DIR>             .
01/19/2023   09:26 PM    <DIR>             ..
01/19/2023   09:26 PM         22,228,536 cmake-gui.exe
01/19/2023   09:26 PM         10,627,640 cmake.exe
01/19/2023   09:26 PM          1,911,352 cmcldeps.exe
01/19/2023   09:26 PM         10,700,344 cpack.exe
```

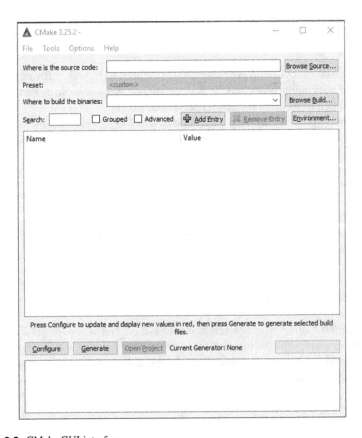

Figure 8-2 CMake GUI interface

```
01/19/2023   09:26 PM          11,552,824 ctest.exe
               5 File(s)       57,020,696 bytes
               2 Dir(s)   504,891,195,392 bytes free


D:\Programs\cmake-3.25.2-x86_64\bin>cmake

Usage

  cmake [options] <path-to-source>
  cmake [options] <path-to-existing-build>
  cmake [options] -S <path-to-source> -B <path-to-build>
```

Specify a source directory to (re-)generate a build system for it in
the current working directory. Specify an existing build directory
to re-generate its build system.

Run 'cmake --help' for more information.

Much more interesting and useful is the subst command, which does not require
administrator rights and allows you to mount a folder as a disk partition, assigning
a given letter to this disk.

8.11   Conclusion

In this chapter, we have discussed the MSYS and MSYS2 packages. They are
intended, in other words, to generate a `Makefile` on the target machine and build
a program or library using the MinGW compiler and utilities included in MSYS
(`make`, `ar`, etc.). For most cases, the first version of MSYS is sufficient (we only
used MSYS2 to build OpenSSL).

The main advantage of MSYS is its compactness and self-sufficiency. MSYS2
is modern, but much more resource intensive. Both versions work great in portable
mode.

It's important to note—although these packages can be used on their own as a
set of useful utilities—they are generally not needed once a program or library has
been built. They are needed at the build stage; their further use is optional.

Compilers

9

This chapter provides brief descriptions of the widely used compilers for C/C++ and Fortran and gives practical advice on working with them.

A compiler is a special program designed to translate code written in a high-level language (Fortran, C/C++, etc.) into a processor "language" consisting of machine instructions. The input of the compiler is (in the simplest case) a file with the text of the program, say, in the C/C++ language, and the output of the compiler generates a binary file containing the object code of the program. Object code in this form is not suitable for running on a machine, since it does not yet have an executable file format, and, moreover, it may contain illegal references to other program units (libraries). Typically, an application consists of several program units (source code files in a high-level language) and can use an external object code library. The compiler will create object files from source code files. The linker links and combines the created object files and external library code into a single application executable file.

Most of the classical compiling languages are implemented exactly according to this scheme (a language implementation primarily means the creation of a compiler of this language). Of course, this does not apply to Java and .NET Framework technologies, since they use a virtual machine to interpret the code they have created, that is, they do not compile code that can be executed by the processor, but code that will be executed on the processor by an intermediate program called an interpreter.[1]

Let us now give a brief overview of modern C/C++ compilers, limiting ourselves to considering only those that, firstly, more or less fully cover the existing standard of C/C++ languages and, secondly, are well-deservedly popular. It is for these

---

[1] Obviously, there is a significant performance penalty, but the advantage of this approach is the relative ease of implementation of cross-platform (portable) applications.

B. I. Tuleuov, A. B. Ospanova, *Beginning C++ Compilers*, https://doi.org/10.1007/978-1-4842-9563-2_9

reasons that we do not consider the once very popular compiler from Watcom[2] and the equally popular compiler from the famous company Borland.[3]

9.1   GCC/MinGW

The GNU C/C++ compiler is part of the GNU Compiler Collection (GCC), which is a set of compilers for C, C++, Objective-C, Fortran, Ada, Java, and Go, as well as libraries for these languages (libstdc++, ...). GCC was originally written as a compiler for GNU operating systems, that is, Unix systems, and only supported the C language; support for other languages was added later. The GNU Project is known to be supported by the Free Software Foundation (FSF), which distributes GCC under the GNU GPL.

As the official compiler of the GNU Project, GCC is the default compiler for many Unix systems. The latest version at the time of this writing is GCC 7.3, released on January 25, 2018.

GCC was originally written primarily in C; however, since August 2012, development is already in C++, and compiler versions above 4.8 require a C++ compiler that supports the ISO/IEC C++03 standard for their assembly.

GCC, perhaps, holds the record for the number of supported processor architectures (more than 75) and operating systems. Under Windows, GCC has been ported under the name MinGW (Minimalist GNU for Windows), which we will now consider.

The GCC interface follows Unix conventions. To compile, users invoke language-specific control programs (driver program, gcc for C, g++ for C++, etc.) that parse command-line arguments, call the appropriate compiler, run an assembler to output the file, and, if required, call the linker, which generates the resulting executable binary file. Each of the compilers is a separate program that reads the source code of the compiled program and produces an object file containing machine code.

MinGW is a port of GCC (GNU Compiler Collection) to the Windows platform. According to some reports, at present the popularity of MinGW (34%) is almost equal to that of the Microsoft C/C++ compiler (36%). The reason for this, in our opinion, is not only the high quality of the compiler and its free usage (the Microsoft C/C++ compiler is included in some products supplied free of charge) but also its availability: MinGW is perhaps the only compiler that can be deployed in literally

---

[2] At present, its successor Open Watcom is being developed by the open source community.

[3] The Borland C/C++ compiler (as well as other products of this company) was, of course, a standout product in some ways, with a friendly development environment bundled with an extended (and non-C++ standard) library. Borland's mediocre policy ruined this compiler (although Embarcadero, which owns the rights to this product, continues to release the C++ Builder line, this environment is not popular). The minimum version of Borland C++ 5.5 after registration can be downloaded free of charge from the Embarcadero website: www.embarcadero.com/free-tools/ccompiler/free-download

five minutes, and then you can start writing code—all you need to do is download an archive of about 45 MB (megabytes!), unpack it, and make minimal settings.

It should also be noted that there used to be an opinion that GCC does not generate the fastest code; however, the latest performance tests show that MinGW is only slightly inferior to the Intel C/C++ compiler in terms of the execution speed of the code generated by the compiler, which is quite understandable (it is interesting to note that at the same time, the speed of these compilers themselves is the lowest, and the Intel C/C++ compiler is the slowest, and this is also quite understandable). The authors were pleasantly surprised to find that MinGW handled the combinatorial task of generating combinations about 10% faster than Microsoft C/C++.

9.1.1 Default Installation

For a traditional installation of the MinGW compiler, download a small web installer, run it, and follow the instructions.

9.1.2 Building from the Sources

Since its source code is freely distributed, MinGW can be compiled by yourself. It is important to keep in mind the following circumstance: GCC (and therefore MinGW) depends on the GMP, MPFR and MPC libraries, and if linked to them dynamically, then the corresponding dynamic libraries must be in the linker library search directories, both when MinGW is built and when using the already built MinGW.

However, it is not our task to teach the user how to build MinGW—excellent builds made by experienced programmers are available from many links that we will give later. Those interested can follow the link: https://gcc.gnu.org/wiki/InstallingGCC.

9.1.3 Easy Installation

As we noted earlier, installing MinGW is extremely easy. The choice is not easy—which of the many MinGW builds to choose for installation? Official and unofficial[4] (the so-called personal builds), there are about a dozen, if not more; it is extremely difficult for an inexperienced user to understand them.

Also confusing is the fact that the user is given a choice of platform (Windows 32 or 64), threading model (posix or win32), and C++ exception handling model (dwarf, sjlj, or SEH). Without going into details, we will briefly describe these technologies in the context of the Windows operating system.

---

[4] In principle, anyone can build MinGW for themselves, since its source code is open.

dwarf (DW2, dwarf-2) is only implemented for 32-bit mode, but it is slightly faster than sjlj (setjmp/longjmp) in the sense that the sjlj technology slows down the program a bit, because it adds some additional exception handling code to each user function, and this code is always executed. However, dwarf injects extra information into the executable for handling exceptions, so the size of the executable grows when compared to using sjlj technology. In defense of sjlj, it should be said that this technology is able to interact to a certain extent with Windows system libraries and libraries created by the Microsoft C/C++ compiler. sjlj cannot catch an exception thrown by code generated by the Microsoft C/C++ compiler, but allows the user to throw their own exceptions through other libraries, as is the case when an exception is thrown in a Windows API callback and caught (handled) in the WinMain function. Let's also add that sjlj is available for both 32-bit and 64-bit mode.

SEH (structured exception handling) is native to Windows, but is only implemented in 64-bit mode due to patent restrictions.

From all of these, we conclude: if possible, use SEH; otherwise, we choose sjlj and try to avoid dwarf.

As for the threading model, we advise you to choose posix, as in this case the generated code will be more conforming to the standard (win32 implements the Windows threading model).

MinGW projects merged into MinGW-W64 after 2013; new builds are available at https://sourceforge.net/projects/mingw-w64/files/. By opening this page and scrolling, you can see direct links to different versions of the compiler. In accordance with the recommendations from Table 9-1, you can select the compiler builds that the user needs. We only recommend that you do not use the MinGW-W64 Online Installer, since the compiler in the form of an unpacked archive is much more convenient for both installation and use. Old builds can be downloaded from https://sourceforge.net/projects/mingwbuilds/files/, the map of which is shown in Figure 9-1.

Let us remind you once again that you can download the compiler using the links provided as a separate 7z archive file, the name of which may contain the 'rev' suffix denoting the build number. The higher the build number, the fresher the compiler.

Setting up the compiler is extremely simple (for the 32-bit version of the compiler, change 64 to 32): unpack the archive to the directory D:\Programs\mingw64. The path to the directory with the compiler executable files, D:\Programs\mingw64\bin, is added to the PATH system variable (it is better to do this in the console).

Table 9-1 MinGW compiler options

Bitness of the Operating System	Thread Models		Exception Handling Models		
	posix	win32	dwarf	sjlj	seh
32: x32, i686	Yes	Yes	Yes	Yes	**No**
64: x64, x86_64	Yes	Yes	**No**	Yes	Yes

```
https://sourceforge.net/projects/mingwbuilds/files/
   external-binary-packages
       Qt-Builds
       README.txt
       msys+7za+wget+svn+git+mercurial+cvs-rev13.7z 2013-05-15 45.1MB
       .  .  .
       msys+7za+wget+svn+git+mercurial+cvs-rev0.7z 2012-05-24 29.8MB
   host-windows
       testing
       releases
           4.8.1
               32-bit
               64-bit
                   threads-win32
                   threads-posix
                       seh
                           x64-4.8.1-release-posix-seh-rev5.7z 2013-08-30 48.3MB
                           .  .  .
                           x64-4.8.1-release-posix-seh-rev0.7z 2013-06-01 35.6MB
                       sjlj
           .  .  .
           4.6.2
       repository.txt
   mingw-sources
   mingw-builds-install
   mingw-builds-sources
   external-sources-packages
   host-linux
   host-osx
```

Figure 9-1 MinGW and MSYS tree

Next, as in the case of MSYS, you need to create a batch file `mingw481.bat` to start MinGW:

```
@echo off

set PATH=%~d0\Programs\mingw64-4.8.1\bin;%PATH%
```

and place this file in the `Programs\bin` directory.

Note Since it is often necessary to have different versions of the compiler on hand, we advise you to unpack archives of different versions of the MinGW compiler into folders like `mingw64-x.x.x`, where `x.x.x` means the compiler version.

For example, for the `mingw64-8.1.0` version, we create a batch file `mingw81.bat` in the `Programs\bin` folder:

```
@echo off

set PATH=%~d0\Programs\mingw64-8.1.0\bin;%PATH%
```

Note If you try to run an executable file created by the MinGW compiler through the Windows Explorer, you can get an error message about the absence of some dlls. This happens when step 2 is omitted. The reason for the error is that these dlls are located just in the `D:\Programs\mingw64\bin` directory.

However, even if these libraries are available, it makes no sense to run console (without a graphical interface) programs from under Explorer—a command-line window opens to execute the program, the program is executed, and then the window immediately closes after program termination, so looking and reading something is practically impossible. Such a peculiar sense of humor among Windows developers.

There are also great builds of newer versions of MinGW supported by enthusiasts. All of them are distributed as archives; they do not require installation.

Builds of new versions of MinGW in various combinations can be downloaded from https://winlibs.com.

```
UCRT runtime
  GCC 12.2.0 + LLVM/Clang/LLD/LLDB 15.0.7 + MinGW-w64 10.0.0 (UCRT)
      - release 4   (LATEST)
    Win32: 7-Zip archive* | Zip archive   -   without
        LLVM/Clang/LLD/LLDB: 7-Zip archive* | Zip archive
    Win64: 7-Zip archive* | Zip archive   -   without
        LLVM/Clang/LLD/LLDB: 7-Zip archive* | Zip archive

MSVCRT runtime
  GCC 12.2.0 + LLVM/Clang/LLD/LLDB 15.0.7 + MinGW-w64 10.0.0 (MSVCRT)
      - release 4   (LATEST)
    Win32: 7-Zip archive* | Zip archive   -   without
        LLVM/Clang/LLD/LLDB: 7-Zip archive* | Zip archive
    Win64: 7-Zip archive* | Zip archive   -   without
        LLVM/Clang/LLD/LLDB: 7-Zip archive* | Zip archive
```

You can download the new MinGW builds from https://github.com/niXman/mingw-builds-binaries/releases too.

```
x86_64-12.2.0-release-posix-seh-msvcrt-rt_v10-rev2.7z 68.1 MB
x86_64-12.2.0-release-posix-seh-ucrt-rt_v10-rev2.7z   68 MB
```

Stephan T. Lavavej, a Principal Software Development Engineer at Microsoft, maintaining Visual Studio's C++ standard library implementation, in his personal website https://nuwen.net/mingw.html supports his MinGW build which he pronounces as "noo-when":

My MinGW distribution ("distro") is x64-native and currently contains GCC 11.2.0 and Boost 1.77.0. `mingw-18.0.exe` (96.9 MB): This is a self-extracting archive. It's incredibly easy to install; see How To Install below. `mingw-18.0-without-git.exe` (49.3 MB): This is smaller, if you've already installed git. My build scripts are available on GitHub, and they're also stored within the distro itself

It is easy to install his build—just unpack it into the `Programs\bin` directory.

Finally, here is the `mingw_all.bat` batch file that will run at once different versions of the MinGW compiler in several tabs, and the Far file manager in one of the tabs of the ConEmu command-line emulator at once different versions of the MinGW compiler and in one of the tabs the file manager Far (Figure 6-4):

```
@echo off
set "C++FILES=C:\User\C++"

start %~d0\Programs\ConEmu-221218\ConEmu64.exe /cmd
    @%~dp0\c++_startfile.txt

REM Switch off the next string for debugging
REM and switch on for release

REM exit
```

The `c++_startfile.txt` file, like `mingw_all.bat`, is located in the `Programs\bin` directory and looks like this:

```
>cmd /k "color 70 && RenameTab 11.2.0/nuwen.net && mingw-nw.bat &&
    PROMPT=$E[32mgcc 11.2.0/nuwen.net@$E\$E[92m$P$E[90m
    $_$E[90m$$$E[m && chcp 65001 > nul && cd /d ++FILES%"
cmd /k "color 02 && RenameTab 12.2.0/niXman && mingw12.bat &&
    PROMPT=$E[32mgcc 12.2.0/niXman@$E\$E[92m$P$E[90m$_$E[90m$ $$E[m
    && chcp 65001 > nul && cd /d %C++FILES%"
cmd /k "color 0A && RenameTab 12.2.0/winlibs.com &&
    mingw12-winlibs.bat && PROMPT=$E[32mgcc
    12.2.0/winlibs.com@$E[92m$P$E[90m$ _$E[90m$$$E[m && chcp 65001
    > nul && cd /d %C++FILES%"
cmd /k "color 09 && RenameTab 8.1.0/niXman && mingw81.bat &&
    PROMPT=$E[32mgcc 8.1.0/niXman@$E\$E[92m$P$E[90m$_$E[90m$ $$E[m &&
    chcp 65001 > nul && cd /d %C++FILES%"
cmd /k "color 00 && RenameTab Far Manager && Far.bat &&
    PROMPT=$E[32mFar Manager@$E\$E[92m$P$E[90m$_$E[90m$$$E[m && chcp
    65001 > nul && cd /d %C++FILES%"
```

The `Far.bat` file (of course, in the folder `Programs\bin`) is the following:

```
@echo off

call %~d0\Programs\Far30b5577_x64\Far.exe

exit
```

9.2   Microsoft C/C++ Optimizing Compiler

The Microsoft C/C++ Optimizing Compiler is one of the most popular compilers for the Windows operating system, which is not surprising given that Microsoft itself is the developer of Windows. It is commercial, although it is possible to use it for free as part of some products with limited functionality (as far as we know, the functionality of the compiler itself in such products is the same as in commercial ones).

Note A common misconception about compilers is that users identify the compiler with the development environment. For example, the question "What compiler do you use?" is often answered with "Visual Studio," "Visual C++," or "Code::Blocks," depending on preference. We remind you once again that the compiler is a command-line utility and does not have a visual interface at all.

Most users deal primarily with the Microsoft C/C++ Optimizing Compiler. The prototype of this compiler, based on Lattice C, was released under the name Microsoft C 1.0 back in 1983 and was, of course, 16 bits. Its further evolution, starting from the hitherto popular 32-bit versions, can be traced from Table A-1 (at a certain stage, Microsoft released a line of Quick products, as if competing with Borland's Turbo products, which included the QuickC integrated environment with the same Microsoft C compiler in composition; they are all 16 bits).

Note It should be noted some terminological liberty: often, referring to the Microsoft C/C++ compiler, they say and write "Visual C++ Compiler," which is not true. The situation is aggravated when it comes to versions. Microsoft itself contributes to the confusion with its inconsistency (e.g., experienced developers remember the situation with the names of WinAPI functions). To avoid confusion, refer to the compiler version, not the product version.

The Microsoft C/C++ compiler executable is `cl.exe`. More precisely, this is not the compiler itself, but a driver utility that controls the compiler and linker. Let's quote the official documentation and make some clarifications [12]:

> You can start this tool only from a Visual Studio developer command prompt. You cannot start it from a system command prompt or from File Explorer. For more information, see Use the MSVC toolset from the command line.
>
> The compilers produce Common Object File Format (COFF) object (`.obj`) files. The linker produces executable (`.exe`) files or dynamic-link libraries (DLLs).
>
> All compiler options are case-sensitive. You may use either a forward slash (`/`) or a dash (`-`) to specify a compiler option.
>
> To compile without linking, use the `/c` option.

Note

- You can start cl.exe not only from a Visual Studio developer command prompt. You can start it from a system command prompt with EWDK. No Visual Studio is needed at all, since the MSVC toolset is contained in EWDK.
- The linker produces also driver (.sys) files, not only executable (.exe) files or dynamic-link libraries (DLLs).

9.2.1 Default Installation

Despite the apparent simplicity (download and install), the process of installing the Microsoft C/C++ compiler is not easy, as you have to make a choice.

For a long time, the Microsoft compiler could be used by installing one of three products: Windows SDK, Windows DDK, and Microsoft Visual Studio. Since in most cases users deal with various editions of the integrated development environment (**IDE**) of Microsoft Visual Studio, which includes a compiler, an advanced code editor, a debugger, and … a lot of rubbish unnecessary for the average user (we are not interested in other languages supported by Visual Studio, as well as technologies such as database support or .NET Framework),[5] then let's talk about the first two packages first.

Starting with version 8, the Windows SDK no longer ships with a complete command-line build environment. The compiler and build environment must be installed separately.

Recent versions of the Windows DDK, now called the Windows Driver Kit (WDK), require Visual Studio and the Windows SDK.

Visual Studio is a commercial product and comes in several editions such as Standard, Professional, and Team System, but Visual Studio Express is free (with reduced features, but the C/C++ compiler is not limited). Starting with the version of Visual Studio 2015, there have been changes; now the product comes in three editions: the free Community Edition, which includes all Express versions, and the paid Professional Edition for small projects and the Enterprise Edition for large projects.

Note that the Visual Studio 2015 distribution "weighs" 3.8 GB, and its installation does not always go smoothly (e.g., even if you install Visual Studio on a drive, say D:\, the installer will definitely require several gigabytes of free space on drive C:\). If you have a slow Internet, then the online installation option may be more suitable for you.

---

[5] We mean the fact that when installing Microsoft Visual Studio, components are installed along the way that are completely unnecessary for C/C++ programming, and these components are often uninstallable.

Released in 2017, Visual Studio 2017 already requires about 7.5 GB to install, and bug fixes are constantly being released (the latest version is 15.6.0, released on March 5, 2018).

In any case, you have to download several gigabytes of data. A natural question arises: Why, in fact, in order to install a C++ compiler, is it necessary to make such sacrifices? Is there a simpler way to install it?

And, in fact, in recent years, the situation has begun to change for the better—finally, Microsoft realized the inferiority of the situation. In 2015, a new product called Microsoft Visual C++ Build Tools 2015 was announced, which is a set of tools (C++ compiler, linker and other auxiliary utilities, libraries and header files, build scripts, and various versions of the Windows SDK, although the latter can also be not installed) to build C++ applications and libraries for desktop versions of Windows, without having to install Visual Studio. This product can already be downloaded from the company's website as a 3 MB web installer. Of course, the online installation option is not suitable for installation on several computers. For offline installation, the downloaded web installer must be run with the /layout key—in this case, the installer will download all the necessary components to the specified directory for subsequent installation in offline mode, but with the /NoWeb key. The total size of the downloaded files is approximately 1.7 GB. Note that this product has a command-line interface—it does not include any visual development environment, not even a simple code editor.

Note We draw readers' attention to the fact that the Microsoft website actively advertises the free Visual Studio Code, which is cross-platform—it can be used on Linux, Mac OS X, or Windows, but this product is just an advanced source code editor and does not contain C/C++ compiler at all in it! It is also worth noting that this editor is based on the well-known Atom editor and is not lightweight: its executable file is about 100 MB in size.

With the release of Visual Studio 2017, one more option to install the C/C++ compiler has been added—now the Visual Studio web installer allows you to choose a C/C++ compiler for installation in the minimum, so to speak, configuration; the volume of downloaded files is about 300–400 MB.

When installing Microsoft Visual Studio, groups of command prompt shortcuts are also installed for compiling and building C/C++ projects from the command line. Table 9-2 gives a brief description of them for Visual Studio 2010 and Visual Studio 2015 versions (the item marked with an asterisk only performs compilation).

It should be noted that Microsoft has recently been actively promoting the new MSBuild build system, trying to replace the traditional nmake build utility.[6]

---

[6] Recall again that Windows does not have a make utility, and nmake is its counterpart; however, these utilities are not compatible.

Table 9-2 Visual Studio
command prompt shortcuts

Product	Command-Line Shortcut Name
Visual Studio 2015	Developer Command Prompt for VS2015*
	MSBuild Command Prompt for VS2015
	VS2015 x86 Native Tools Command Prompt
	VS2015 x64 Native Tools Command Prompt
	VS2015 x86 x64 Cross Tools Command Prompt
	VS2015 x64 x86 Cross Tools Command Prompt
VS 2010	Visual Studio Command Prompt (2010)
	Visual Studio x64 Win64 Command Prompt (2010)

9.2.2   Easy Installation (Without Visual Studio) with EWDK

According to the Microsoft website, given the high cost (in terms of labor) of individual installations of Visual Studio 2015 and WDK for organizations with a large number of developers, they released a special version of the already mentioned Windows Driver Kit (WDK) called Enterprise Windows Driver Kit (Enterprise WDK),[7] based on Visual Studio 2015 Enterprise edition, WDK, and Windows SDK. The Enterprise WDK also does not include a visual development environment—only a command-line interface is offered. The first version of Enterprise WDK includes

- Visual Studio Build Tools, C/C++ compiler, linker, and object libraries (lib) from Visual Studio build 14.00.24720.0 (VS 2015 Update 1)
- Windows SDK build 10586.13
- .NET Framework 4.6 SDK build 10586.13
- Windows Driver Development Kit build 10586.0

Thus, the Enterprise WDK contains everything you need to build drivers and basic test Win32 applications. The installation of the product is extremely simple—in accordance with the stated goals, it comes in the form of a single zip file, which you just need to unzip and run the setup script as an administrator.

Later, the Enterprise WDK has also been significantly updated—starting from version 1709, this package now comes in the form of a massive ISO file, approximately 5.4 GB in size, and does not require installation; only easy configuration is needed. At the time of the release of this product (2018), this package provided the easiest way to install the described compiler, despite the need to download 5.4 GB of data; by now, unfortunately, the file size has grown by about three times; we will describe this method as follows.

---

[7] http://msdn.microsoft.com/windows/hardware/drivers/develop/installing-the-enterprise-wdk

Table 9-3 Enterprise Windows Driver Kit (EWDK) downloads

#	OS Version	EWDK Version	Visual Studio Build Tools Version	Size, GB	Format	Link
1	Windows 10	1607	VS 2015, 2015	1.8	zip	[17]
2	Windows 10	1703	VS 2015, 2015	1.9	zip	[17]
3	Windows 10	1709	VS 2017, 15.2	7.3	ISO	[18]
4	Windows 10	1709	VS 2017, 15.4	5.3	ISO	[18]
5	Windows 10	1709	VS 2017, 15.6	5.5	ISO	[18]
6	Windows 10	1803	VS 2017, 15.6	5.6	ISO	[18]
7	Windows 10	1803	VS 2017, 15.7	8.4	ISO	[18]
8	Windows 10	1809	VS 2017, 15.8	12.7	ISO	[18]
9	Windows 10	1809	VS 2017, 15.8.9	12.7	ISO	[18]
10	Windows 10	1903	VS 2019, 16.0	12.4	ISO	[19]
11	Windows 10	2004	VS 2019, 16.7	12.3	ISO	[19]
12	Windows Server 2022		VS 2019, 16.9.2	15.7	ISO	[19]
13	Windows 11	21H2	VS 2019, 16.9.2	16.0	ISO	[20]
			VS 2019, 16.11.10			
14	Windows 11	22H2	VS 2022, 17.1.5	15.8	ISO	[21]

Enterprise Windows Driver Kit (EWDK) downloads: The current version of EWDK can be downloaded from the official Microsoft website at [16]. Links to previous versions are given in Table 9-3.

We recommend unpacking the `zip` version of EWDK into a folder, say `Programs\EWDK-vxxx`. The ISO version of the toolkit should be handled in a slight different way: this ISO file must be mounted as a virtual DVD disk. Windows 10 Explorer can mount such files itself, but Windows 7 Explorer cannot. Sometimes, the context menu item of Explorer for mounting ISO files is intercepted by another software, for example, archivers or UltraISO, and then it is useful to use third-party mounting tools. One of the best software of this kind is WinCDEmu (https://wincdemu.sysprogs.org), an open source CD/DVD/BD emulator which runs on 32-bit and 64-bit Windows versions from XP to Windows 10.

Mounting the ISO file with the aid of WinCDEmu or such software under Windows 7 requires an administrator privilege. However, there is workaround here which doesn't require such restriction. For this, one should extract the content of the ISO file into some directory, say, `Programs\EWDK-vxxx`. Then this folder should be mounted as a disk with the aid of the `subst` command:

```
subst X: D:\Programs\EWDK-vxxx
```

Note Notice that, in this case, the extracted content can be edited, which gives some extra flexibility.

Reducing EWDK size: Unfortunately, EWDK is too fat. Besides, if you need things related only to the C/C++ compiler, then EWDK can be greatly facilitated. And if you are going to write code that is intended only for one processor platform, say, Intel, the size of the EWDK can be reduced to 5.5 GB; we will talk about this in more detail now.

In the following example, the EWDK is mounted on drive F:. Using the `ncdu` utility, let's examine the EWDK directory structure in terms of disk space occupied.

```
--- /f --------------------------------------------------------------
   15.7 GiB [#########################] /Program Files
  228.0 KiB [                         ]  LICENSE.rtf
   12.0 KiB [                         ] /Utilities
   10.0 KiB [                         ] /BuildEnv
    2.0 KiB [                         ]  LaunchBuildEnv.cmd
    2.0 KiB [                         ]  Version.txt

--- /f/Program Files ------------------------------------------------
   12.6 GiB [#########################] /Microsoft Visual Studio
    3.0 GiB [######                   ] /Windows Kits
   45.3 MiB [                         ] /Reference Assemblies
   28.2 MiB [                         ] /Microsoft SDKs
    2.1 MiB [                         ]  ucrtbased.dll
   24.0 KiB [                         ] /Microsoft

--- /f/Program Files/Microsoft Visual Studio/2022/BuildTools/VC/Tools
   10.8 GiB [#########################] /MSVC
  104.9 MiB [                         ] /Llvm

--- /f/Program Files/Microsoft
        Visual Studio/2022/BuildTools/VC/Tools/MSVC/14.31.31103 --------------
    6.2 GiB [#########################] /lib
    4.1 GiB [################         ] /atlmfc
  388.0 MiB [#                        ] /bin
   18.3 MiB [                         ] /include
    5.5 MiB [                         ] /crt
   90.0 KiB [                         ] /Auxiliary
```

The acronym `atlmfc` refers to the Active Template Library (ATL) and Microsoft Foundation Classes (MFC) packages developed by Microsoft. ATL, for example, is a set of C++ template classes to make it easier to write COM components (COM objects, OLE automation servers, and ActiveX controls). MFC is designed to create Windows GUI applications and consists of many C++ classes. These packages are traditionally included with Visual Studio.

Both libraries, of course, have nothing to do with the C++ standard and are intended exclusively for Windows. In addition, these libraries are not very popular—for example, Microsoft's own product Microsoft Word, as well as other components of the Microsoft Office package, is written without using the MFC library at all!

By excluding the `atlmfc` folder from copying, we can reduce the size of the copied files by 4.1 GB. Fortunately, the `robocopy` utility can specify folders that should not be copied:

```
robocopy SOURCE DEST /mir /xd path_or_folder_to_exclude
```

If you want to exclude the folder `"F:\Program Files\Microsoft Visual Studio\2022\BuildTools\VC\Tools\MSVC\14.31 .31103\atlmfc\"` from being copied, then you, probably, type

```
robocopy F:\ J:\Programs\EWDK\ /mir /xd "F:\Program Files\Microsoft
    Visual Studio\2022\BuildTools\VC\Tools\MSVC\14.31.31103\atlmfc\"

------------------------------------------------------------------

              Total    Copied   Skipped  Mismatch    FAILED    Extras
    Dirs  :    3903      3902         1         0         0         0
    Files :   33737     33737         0         0         0         0
    Bytes :  15.636 g  15.636 g       0         0         0         0
    Times :  0:06:40   0:05:17                        0:00:00   0:01:22


    Speed :              52820176 Bytes/sec.
    Speed :              3022.394 MegaBytes/min.
    Ended : Wednesday, April 5, 2023 11:53:45 AM


D:\Users\John>
```

As you can see, despite the option not to copy the specified folder, the utility copied the entire directory tree. `robocopy` is extremely fast, but unfortunately a big accuracy is needed when you deal with this utility. Notice the trailing slash in the exclude path; as soon as we remove it, the utility works as it should:

```
robocopy F:\ J:\Programs\EWDK\ /mir /xd "F:\Program Files\Microsoft
    Visual Studio\2022\BuildTools\VC\Tools\MSVC\14.31.31103\atlmfc\"
------------------------------------------------------------------

              Total    Copied   Skipped  Mismatch    FAILED    Extras
    Dirs  :    3757      3755         2         0         0         0
    Files :   32006     32006         0         0         0         0
    Bytes :  11.501 g  11.501 g       0         0         0         0
    Times :  0:04:31   0:03:20                        0:00:00   0:01:10


    Speed :              61570838 Bytes/sec.
    Speed :              3523.111 MegaBytes/min.
    Ended : Wednesday, April 5, 2023 12:36:46 PM


D:\Users\John>
```

To exclude a folder from copying, you can specify only its name, and not the full path to this folder: instead of F:\Program Files\Microsoft Visual Studio\2022\BuildTools\VC\Tools\MSVC\14.31.31103\atlmfc, you can specify atlmfc, and in this case the result will be the same:

```
robocopy F:\ J:\Programs\EWDK\ /mir /xd atlmfc
------------------------------------------------------------------

              Total     Copied   Skipped  Mismatch    FAILED     Extras
   Dirs :      3757       3755         2         0         0          0
  Files :     32006      32006         0         0         0          0
  Bytes :   11.501 g   11.501 g        0         0         0          0
  Times :   0:04:30    0:03:17                         0:00:00    0:01:12


  Speed :              62638208 Bytes/sec.
  Speed :              3584.187 MegaBytes/min.
  Ended : Wednesday, April 5, 2023 12:26:18 PM


D:\Users\John>
```

Note It should be remembered that if only the folder name is specified for exclusion when copying, all folders with the same name in the directory tree of the copied folder will be excluded from the copy list.

The following are the details of copying to a Flash stick formatted with the NTFS file system: pay attention to the copying time.

```
------------------------------------------------------------------

              Total     Copied   Skipped  Mismatch    FAILED     Extras
   Dirs :      3757       3756         1         0         0          0
  Files :     32006      32006         0         0         0          0
  Bytes :   11.501 g   11.501 g        0         0         0          0
  Times :   1:20:01    1:08:16                         0:00:00    0:11:44


  Speed :              3015037 Bytes/sec.
  Speed :              172.521 MegaBytes/min.
  Ended : Friday, April 7, 2023 3:21:43 PM


C:\Users\User>
```

Now we can mount the directory with the EWDK files as a virtual drive using the subst utility. Note that this does not require administrator rights at all!

```
subst X: J:\Programs\EWDK

D:\Users\John>X:

X:\>dir
 Volume in drive X is DATA
 Volume Serial Number is 5E81-8465
```

```
Directory of X:\

04/05/2023  12:36 PM    <DIR>          .
04/05/2023  12:36 PM    <DIR>          ..
08/06/2022  04:57 AM    <DIR>          BuildEnv
08/06/2022  04:52 AM             52 LaunchBuildEnv.cmd
08/06/2022  04:52 AM        231,551 LICENSE.rtf
08/06/2022  04:57 AM    <DIR>          Program Files
08/06/2022  04:57 AM    <DIR>          Utilities
08/06/2022  04:52 AM             38 Version.txt
               3 File(s)        231,641 bytes
               5 Dir(s)  66,801,131,520 bytes free

X:\>
```

Finally, note that if you develop programs for, say, only Intel processors, then you can also throw out support for processors of other architectures: Arm, Arm64, Arm64ec, and CHPE. As a result, the size of the package will be reduced to 5.484 GB, that is, 10 GB can be saved. The corresponding command is given as follows. We copy the optimized directory tree to the Programs\EWDK_COMPACT directory:

```
D:\Users>robocopy F:\ J:\Programs\EWDK_COMPACT\ /mir /xd atlmfc arm
    arm64 arm64ec chpe

--------------------------------------------------------------------

               Total    Copied   Skipped  Mismatch    FAILED    Extras
    Dirs :      3373      3253       120         0         0         0
   Files :     27730     27730         0         0         0         0
   Bytes :    5.484 g   5.484 g         0         0         0         0
   Times :   0:09:55   0:08:36                         0:00:00   0:01:19


   Speed :              11394562 Bytes/sec.
   Speed :               652.002 MegaBytes/min.
   Ended : Wednesday, April 12, 2023 11:23:13 AM


D:\Users>
```

Now here are the details of copying to a Flash card again, this time formatted with the exFAT file system: copying time has increased, while only about 5.5 GB of data is copied.

```
C:\Users\John>robocopy D:\ E:\Programs\EWDK_COMPACT\ /mir /xd atlmfc
    arm arm64 arm64ec chpe
--------------------------------------------------------------------

               Total    Copied   Skipped  Mismatch    FAILED    Extras
    Dirs :      3373      3253       120         0         0         0
   Files :     27730     27730         0         0         0         0
   Bytes :    5.484 g   5.484 g         0         0         0         0
   Times :   1:27:25   0:59:21                         0:00:00   0:28:04
```

```
Speed :              1653547 Bytes/sec.
Speed :               94.616 MegaBytes/min.
Ended : Wednesday, April 12, 2023 1:53:45 PM
```

```
C:\Users\John>
```

Again, mount the folder with the optimized EWDK, mount it as a disk, and work:

```
C:\Users\John>subst X: E:\Programs\EWDK_COMPACT
```

9.2.3   Using Microsoft C/C++ Compiler with EWDK

Using the Microsoft C/C++ compiler with EWDK is quite straightforward; just
create batch file vc.bat of the following content:

```
@echo off
set BIT=%1
if "%BIT%" == "32" set VER=86
if "%BIT%" == "64" set VER=64
set "VSROOT=X:\Program Files"
set "WDKVER=10.0.22621.0"
set "BUILDTOOLSPATH=%VSROOT%\Microsoft Visual Studio\2022\BuildTools"
set "WDKROOT=%VSROOT%\Windows Kits\10"
set "WDKLIB=%WDKROOT%\Lib\%WDKVER%"
call "%BUILDTOOLSPATH%\VC\Auxiliary\Build\vcvars%BIT%.bat"
set "INCLUDE=%WDKROOT%\Include\%WDKVER%\ucrt;%INCLUDE%"
set "LIB=%WDKLIB%\ucrt\x%VER%;%WDKLIB%\um\x%VER%;%LIB%"
```

and put it into the Programs\bin directory. To use, perform the next command
on the command line:

```
E:\User\C++>Programs\bin\vc[.bat] 32 | 64
```

Next, you can use the C/C++ compiler:

```
E:\User\C++>vc 64
**********************************************************************
** Visual Studio 2022 Developer Command Prompt v17.1.5
** Copyright (c) 2022 Microsoft Corporation
**********************************************************************
[vcvarsall.bat] Environment initialized for: 'x64'

E:\User\C++>cl
Microsoft (R) C/C++ Optimizing Compiler Version 19.31.31107 for x64
Copyright (C) Microsoft Corporation.  All rights reserved.

usage: cl [ option... ] filename... [ /link linkoption... ]
```

or Microsoft Macro Assembler:

```
E:\User\Asm>ml | ml64


E:\User\Asm>ml64
Microsoft (R) Macro Assembler (x64) Version 14.31.31107.0
Copyright (C) Microsoft Corporation.  All rights reserved.
```

```
usage: ML64 [ options ] filelist [ /link linkoptions]
Run "ML64 /help" or "ML64 /?" for more info
```

9.2.4   Microsoft C/C++ Compiler Options

C/C++ compiler options can be set either through the development environment (IDE) or on the command line. In the first case, the compiler options are set for each project, using the Property Pages dialog box. In the left pane, select Configuration Properties, C/C++, then Compiler Options. Each compiler option has a detailed usage note (hints). For the command line, the `cl.exe` compiler options can be set in three ways:

- Directly on the command line
- Via an auxiliary command file
- Via environment variable CL

The options defined in the CL environment variable are used each time the CL command is invoked. If a command file is used in the CL environment variable or directly on the command line, then the options defined in the command file are used. Unlike the command line or the CL environment variable, a command file can contain multiple lines of options and file names.

Compiler options are processed in "left-to-right" order, and in the event of a conflict, the most recent (rightmost) option takes precedence. The CL environment variable is parsed before command-line options, and in case of conflict, the command-line options take precedence.

The syntax for calling the CL command is

```
CL [option...] file... [option | file ]... [lib...]
    [@command-file] [/link link-opt...]
```

Table 9-4 describes the CL command options.

You can specify any number of options, file names, and libraries, while the number of characters on the command line should not exceed 1024—this limit is imposed by the operating system.

CL command file: A command file is a text file containing many options and file names that could be set directly on the command line or via the CL environment variable. The command file specified in the CL environment variable or command line is treated as an argument. As noted, a command file can contain multiple lines of options and file names, which is not possible with the command line or the CL environment variable.

Options and file names in a command file are parsed according to the location of the command file name in the CL environment variable or command line. However, if the /link option is encountered in the command file, then all remaining options on the line are passed to the linker. Options on subsequent lines in the command

Table 9-4 CL command-line options

Field	Meaning
`option`	One or more CL options. All options apply to all specified source code files. Options are specified using a forward slash ' / ' or a hyphen ' - '. If an option has an argument, then you should clarify in the documentation whether to put a space between the option and the argument. Option names, with the exception of /HELP, are case-sensitive. You can also learn about the order of CL options from the documentation.
`file`	The name of one or more source code files, object (.obj) files, or libraries. CL compiles source code files and passes the names of object files and libraries to the linker.
`lib`	The name of one or more library files. CL passes these names to the linker.
`command-file`	A file containing many options and file names. Details will be described later.
`link-opt`	One or more linker options. CL passes these options to the linker.

file and command-line options following the command file are treated as compiler options.

The command file must not contain the CL command itself. Each option must be located within one line—you cannot break an option into two lines using the backslash character ' \ '.

A command file is recognized by ' @ ' before its name. You can use both absolute and relative paths.

For example, if the following set of options is contained in the file COMFILE

```
/Og /link LIBC.LIB
```

and issues the following command

```
CL /Ob2 @COMFILE MYAPP.C
```

then the final form of the CL command will look like this:

```
CL /Ob2 /Og MYAPP.C /link LIBC.LIB
```

It should be noted that the command-line options and command file can be effectively combined.

Environment variables of the CL command: In addition to the well-known INCLUDE, LIB, and LIBPATH, the CL command also uses the environment variables CL and _CL_ if they are defined. In this case, during processing, the options and arguments defined in the CL environment variable are placed in front, and those defined in the _CL_ environment variable are placed behind the arguments specified on the command line.

The environment variables CL or _CL_ are set as follows:

```
SET CL=[[option] ... [file] ...] [/link link-opt ...]
SET _CL_=[[option] ... [file] ...] [/link link-opt ...]
```

The options and arguments for the CL and _CL_ variables are the same options for the compiler.

These environment variables can be used to set the most commonly used files and options. The CL and _CL_ variables are also limited to 1024 characters (the command-line input limit).

You cannot use the /D option to define a character using the equal sign '='. The number sign '#' can be used instead of the equal sign. Thus, you can use the CL or _CL_ environment variables to define preprocessor constants with explicit values, for example, to define DEBUG=1, use /DDEBUG#1.

Here's an example of using the CL environment variable:

```
SET CL=/Zp2 /Ox /I\INCLUDE\MYINCLS \LIB\BINMODE.OBJ
```

If we now enter the command

```
CL INPUT.C
```

on the command line, the resulting command will be

```
CL /Zp2 /Ox /I\INCLUDE\MYINCLS \LIB\BINMODE.OBJ INPUT.C
```

In the following example, a simple command CL will compile the source files FILE1.c and FILE2.c, then link the object files FILE1.obj, FILE2.obj, and FILE3.obj:

```
SET CL=FILE1.C FILE2.C
SET_CL_=FILE3.OBJ
CL
```

The same can be achieved by running the following command on the command line:

```
CL FILE1.C FILE2.C FILE3.OBJ
```

Note There are situations where it is not possible to directly set compiler options on the command line (e.g., when building drivers or other Visual Studio projects using the new MSBuild build utility). The only (almost) way out in this situation is to use the environment variables of the command CL [11].

9.2.5 Using MSBuild with EWDK

On Section 4.2.3 (page 27), we have described MSBuild usage regardless of the installation method. Now we will clarify the details of using this utility. Those users who have Visual Studio installed can simply launch the appropriate command line from the Visual Studio start menu, but here, since we are describing work without using Visual Studio, we will explain how to use the MSBuild utility using the EWDK.

After mounting the EWDK ISO disk or folder Programs\EWDK_COMPACT (Programs\EWDK) to a virtual disk, say X:, we have two choices:

1. If we want to compile programs in standard C/C++ languages, we run the vc.bat file we wrote and work.

2. If we need to work with the MSBuild utility, then perform the following instructions.

According to Microsoft, we should run `LaunchBuildEnv.cmd` in the root of the disk where EWDK disk or folder is mounted to launch the build environment (command line) [22]. Internally, `LaunchBuildEnv.cmd` calls another batch script, `BuildEnv\SetupBuildEnv.cmd`, in accordance with its command-line parameter. It should be noticed that Microsoft says nothing about the parameter of the command LaunchBuildEnv.cmd: it is merely absent. By default (without any parameter), a 32-bit build environment is launched; to run a 64-bit one, you should execute

```
LaunchBuildEnv.cmd amd64
```

The parameter set includes the values `'x86'`, `'x86_amd64'`, `'amd64'`, `'x86_arm'`, and `'x86_arm64'` and an empty string which is the default and coincides with the `'x86'`, that is, 32-bit environment.

MSBuild can now be run from this build environment; let's consider using this utility in more detail. As we already said, the build process is initiated by the command

```
Msbuild Project.vcxproj /p:Configuration=[Release | Debug]
    /p:Platform=[arm | Win32 | x64]
```

It sometimes lacks some parameters to build sucessfully a project. For such situations, Microsoft suggests to use the so-called `.rsp` (response) files [23]:

> Response (`.rsp`) files are text files that contain MSBuild.exe command-line switches. Each switch can be on a separate line or all switches can be on one line. Comment lines are prefaced with a # symbol. The @ switch is used to pass another response file to MSBuild.exe.

There is also a so-called *Autoresponse* file `MSBuild.rsp` located in the same directory as MSBuild.exe. One can edit this file to include common (default) command-line parameters to MSBuild.exe. These parameters will be applied for all solutions and projects being built.

From version 15.6 and higher, MSBuild searches a project's parent directories for a file `Directory.Build.rsp`. Settings from this file will be applied to all projects in parent directories.

Note If using these files, `MSBuild.rsp` and `Directory.Build.rsp`, are not desirable for some reasons in some cases of MSBuild invocation, one should use the `noAutoResponse` command-line switch. Other response files included explicitly with the @ sign on the command line are processed in a usual way.

```
Msbuild Solution.sln /p:Configuration=Release /p:Platform=x64
    @File.rsp
```

Table 9-5 Platform Toolset values

Visual Studio Version	Platform Toolset Value
Visual Studio .NET 2002	Platform Toolset = `'v70'`
Visual Studio .NET 2003	Platform Toolset = `'v71'`
Visual Studio 2005	Platform Toolset = `'v80'`
Visual Studio 2008	Platform Toolset = `'v90'`
Visual Studio 2010	Platform Toolset = `'v100'`
Visual Studio 2012	Platform Toolset = `'v110'`
Visual Studio 2013	Platform Toolset = `'v120'`
Visual Studio 2015	Platform Toolset = `'v140'`
Visual Studio 2017	Platform Toolset = `'v141'`
Visual Studio 2019	Platform Toolset = `'v142'`
Visual Studio 2022	Platform Toolset = `'v143'`

Sometimes, the `PlatformToolset` property of the MSBuild utility is used to set specific libraries and tools, especially for drivers. One can set `PlatformToolset` without changing the `.vcxproj` file. The user should overwrite the `PlatformToolset` property with `/p:PlatformToolset=v143` to change the toolset, for example:

```
Msbuild MyProject.vcxproj /p:PlatformToolset=v143
```

Platform Toolset values for different versions of Visual Studio are given in Table 9-5.

9.3   Intel C/C++ Optimizing Compiler

The Intel C/C++ compiler, along with the Intel Fortran compiler, is included in various editions (Cluster Edition, Professional Edition, and Composer Edition) of Intel Parallel Studio XE, as well as products such as Intel System Studio and Intel Bi-Endian Compiler (http://software.intel.com/en-us/c-compilers, http://software. intel.com/en-us/fortran-compilers).

Intel Parallel Studio XE includes a variety of C++/Fortran HPC tools and tools for Windows, Linux, and Mac OS X platforms.

Intel System Studio is designed for mobile and embedded C++ development on Windows, Android, and Linux platforms.

Both of these packages additionally include various build tools, such as libraries, tools for creating and debugging multithreaded code, and performance analysis.

The Intel Bi-Endian Compiler is a C++ compiler that uses a single code base for both big-endian (which is the standard for TCP/IP protocols, often referred to as network endian for this reason) and for little-endian (Intel processors usually use this byte order) architectures.

Except for Intel Bi-Endian C++ Compiler, Intel C/C++ compilers are not available separately.

The main feature of this compiler is the support of several high-level optimization methods: Intel is one of the leaders in the processor market, and most IBM

PC–compatible computers use Intel processors. Among the accompanying tools supplied by Intel, we note the Threading Building Blocks (TBB) library, designed for parallel programming on multicore processors, and the Intel Math Kernel Library (MKL), which is a highly optimized implementation of mathematical functions for scientific, engineering, and financial calculations specifically for Intel processors.

We also mention the IMSL Fortran Numerical Library from Rogue Wave— the seventh version of this commercial library, which has more than 40 years of history, comes under Windows with the Fortran version of Intel Parallel Studio XE Composer Edition or as a separate additional product of Rogue Wave IMSL Fortran Libraries. AQPlease check if the phrase "additional product of Rogue Wave" is okay as edited.

As one of the leading vendors, Intel makes sure that its products meet the ever-increasing demands of the computer industry, so Intel compilers fully support parallel programming technologies such as MPI and OpenMP.

The Intel C/C++ compiler can be called in the console with the `icc` or `icl` commands; more detailed information can be obtained from the very rich documentation supplied with the product. Again, the Intel compiler is available for Windows, Mac OS X, Linux, and Intel-based Android devices.

The Intel C/C++ compiler easily integrates into popular development environments such as Visual Studio, Eclipse, Xcode, and Android Studio; it is compatible with popular compilers such as Microsoft C/C++ (Windows) and GCC (Linux, Mac OS X, and Android)

The Intel Fortran Compiler 16.0 fully supports the Fortran ISO/IEC 1539-1:2004 (Fortran 2003) language standard and also provides full support for previous Fortran 95, Fortran 90, Fortran 77, and Fortran IV (Fortran 66) standards for backward compatibility of programs written in accordance with these versions of the standards. In some cases, special compiler options may be required to ensure compatibility with previous versions of the Fortran language standard.

The Intel Fortran Compiler 16.0 also supports many of the innovations of the current Fortran language standard, Fortran 2008 (ISO/IEC 1539-1:2010). Moreover, ISO/IEC TS 29113:2012 (further interoperability with C language), which is part of the future Fortran 2015 standard, is fully supported, and additional innovations of the Fortran 2008 standard are planned for implementation in future versions of the compiler.

Under Windows, Intel Fortran 16.0 integrates seamlessly into Microsoft Visual Studio, and in the console, it can be called with the `ifort` command. Intel Fortran Compiler 16.0 is also available for Windows, Linux, and Mac OS X platforms.

The main disadvantage of this compiler is that it is not free. However, special licenses are offered for students, academic researchers, teachers, and developers of open source programs (Open Source): http://software.intel.com/en-us/articles/non-commercial-software-development. Under these licenses, some Intel products, including compilers, may be used for noncommercial purposes.

We also note that very often Intel C/C++ and Intel Fortran compilers for Linux are installed on clusters and supercomputers (usually, these are the leading corporate distributions of Red Hat Enterprise Linux and SUSE Linux Enterprise Server or their clones).

9.4   Conclusion

In this chapter, we have described in detail how to quickly install the MinGW and Microsoft C/C++ compilers. At the same time, we emphasized that the proposed method of working with the Microsoft C/C++ compiler is described in the technical literature for the first time (Microsoft itself documents the use of EWDK only for working with standard Visual Studio projects and solutions using the MSBuild utility), so the information provided by us are unique.

The technical literature describes the standard installation of MinGW compilers, which is often associated with version conflicts (with the standard method, it is not easy for the average user to install several versions of MinGW and use it). The approach we have taken allows us to use multiple versions of the MinGW and Microsoft C/C++ compilers without any problems.

It is interesting to note that Visual Studio 2022 cannot be installed on Windows 7 SP1, but the included Microsoft C/C++ compiler can be used on Windows 7 SP1 using our method.

Libraries

10

In this chapter, we will talk about static and dynamic-link libraries and how to create them. We will also show that, contrary to popular belief, you do not need the Visual Studio compiler to create such libraries using the Microsoft C/C++ compiler.

10.1   Dynamic and Static Libraries

In this subsection, we will describe how to build libraries for different systems and platforms.

General ways of using libraries: Most of the libraries we are looking at are free software (open source), which, as a rule, are supplied in source code. To use such libraries in your applications, the source code of these libraries must be used in one way or another in your project.[1] Three such ways can be specified; note their advantages and disadvantages:

1. Compiling the source code of the library as a statically linked library: In this case, the library source code is compiled into object files, which are then archived into a so-called static library using a special utility. When used, this static library is linked by a linker with the source code of the application that uses this library into the resulting executable file. At the same time, the initial library code is compiled (used) only once; after building a static library and installing it, the source code of the library can be removed altogether. During the build process of an application that uses this library, all the code used from the library in binary form is included in the generated resulting executable file, so after the application is built, the static library is no longer needed (for the built application!). You only need to distribute one executable file. However, if the source code of the library changes, if the user

---

[1] Sometimes, the source code of an application, when it consists of several files, is called a project.

© The Author(s), under exclusive license to APress Media, LLC,
part of Springer Nature 2024
B. I. Tuleuov, A. B. Ospanova, *Beginning C++ Compilers*,
https://doi.org/10.1007/978-1-4842-9563-2_10

wants to use a new version of it, it may be necessary[2] to rebuild both the static library and the application. Naturally, once a static library is built, it can later be used to build other applications.

For GCC/MinGW compilers, these libraries have the extension $*.a$, and for the Microsoft C/C++ compiler, they have the extension $*.lib$.

2. Compiling the source code of the library as a dynamically linked library: In this case, the library source code is compiled into object files, from which the linker then creates a so-called dynamic library. When you build an application that uses a library, the library's code is not included in the application; the application only "knows" where the required code from the library is located—in the dynamically linked library. This library is used only at runtime, when the application starts. In this case, the executable file loader automatically loads the dynamic-link library file into the address space of the application being launched, after making the necessary settings. From what has been said, it follows that along with the application, you should also distribute the dynamic library file.[3] However, unlike the previous case, when changing the library source code, as a rule, there is no need to rebuild the application itself—it is enough just to rebuild the library source code. Note that many commercial libraries are supplied without source code, in the built, ready-to-use form of dynamically linked libraries. Such libraries have the extension $*.so$ on Linux and $*.dll$ on Windows.

3. Inclusion of the source code of the library in the composition of the source code of the built application: This method is perhaps the most difficult and sophisticated, but, in our opinion, the most flexible. In this case, there is no need to separately build the source code of the library—the entire application is built at once; in addition, the portability (cross-platform) of the code is increased, since the source code has a high degree of portability. The disadvantage of this method is that there is no universal, canonical way to implement it; it differs for each library. Some libraries make this easy: for example, MathGL can be used in this way by defining the constant MGL_SRC as a compilation flag (parameter). Libraries from Boost can be used in source code: Boost has a special utility that allows you to select from many files with complex dependencies the ones necessary for using one or another library from Boost.

Libraries and object files compiled by different compilers should not be mixed. The ideal case is when both the library and the application using them are built by the same compiler (there can only be differences in versions).

Some distributions like TDM-GCC and MinGW builds allow you to choose how you want to implement the exception handling mechanism. It should be remembered that both the application itself and the linked (statically and dynamically) libraries must be built by the same compiler in order to avoid linking errors. If you change the exception handling mechanism (i.e., if you choose a different compiler distribution

---

[2] For example, the format and signature of a function call from the library may change.

[3] There are applications that use dozens of such libraries.

with a different exception handling mechanism), you must recompile all libraries, mainly because the libgcc shared library is named differently for different exception mechanisms.

Building with GCC/MinGW compilers: Perhaps the easiest and most hassle-free is the case of Unix-like operating systems—as a rule, the entire build process can literally fit in three lines:

```
$ ./configure
$ make
# make install
```

The first command performs preconfiguration before building the application/library to be built. In case of its successful completion, you can run the second command for the build itself. After the successful completion of the build phase, you must run the third command—to install the built application/library to the installation directory. Usually, this step requires superuser rights (note the # prompt sign).

Some applications/libraries require another command to be run after the build step:

```
$ make check
```

or

```
$ make test
```

responsible for checking or testing the compiled application/library.

Since GCC runs on Unix systems usually in the bash console serving as a shell, MinGW also requires bash to build many libraries that use GNU utilities. As we have already described, these utilities, including bash, are available in the MSYS package. Therefore, after starting the Windows command line, you must sequentially issue commands

```
> mingw.bat
> bash
```

then execute the standard, already mentioned, build commands.

It should be borne in mind that when building using MSYS with the make install command from under bash, the header files and the finished built library are copied (installed) to the subdirectories of the MSYS tree local/include and local/lib, respectively (initially, there is no local directory in MSYS; it is created after the first make install command).

10.2 Building Libraries

The wonderful book [24, page 72] provides an example of creating static and dynamic libraries in C using GCC, for only Unix-like systems, but we will take this example as a basis, and we will create such libraries already in C++ using both MinGW and Microsoft C/C++ compilers on Windows. Examples of using the created libraries will be illustrated in the next chapter.

Note MSYS and MSYS2 are optional to compile, build, and archive the object files for the following examples.

Let there be two files, `hellofirst.cpp` and `hellosecond.cpp`:

```
/* hellofirst.cpp */

#include <iostream>

using namespace std;

void hellofirst(){
    cout << "The first hello\n";
}
```

```
/* hellosecond.cpp */

#include <iostream>

using namespace std;

void hellosecond(){
    cout << "The second hello\n";
}
```

These two files only contain functions that can be called from another program, `twohellos.cpp`:

```
/* twohellos.cpp */

void hellofirst(void);
void hellosecond(void);

int main(){
  hellofirst();
  hellosecond();

  return(0);
}
```

10.3   Creating User Libraries

Static libraries: Let's first look at creating static libraries with MinGW. With the command[4]

```
g++ -c hellofirst.cpp hellosecond.cpp
```

---

[4] The `-c` option tells the compiler to create an object file with a `.o` extension as output.

we compile the files `hellofirst.cpp` and `hellosecond.cpp` to create object files `hellofirst.o` and `hellosecond.o`. After that, using the `ar` archive utility, we create the `libhello.a` object library:

```
ar -r libhello.a hellofirst.o hellosecond.o
```

In the case of the Microsoft C/C++ compiler, a static library is created in much the same way; only the compiler and linker call format differs.

Compile the files `hellofirst.cpp` and `hellosecond.cpp` to create object files `hellofirst.obj` and `hellosecond.obj`:

```
cl /c hellofirst.cpp hellosecond.cpp
```

Now we use the `lib` utility to combine the created object files into a library `libhello.lib`:

```
lib /out:libhello.lib hellofirst.obj hellosecond.obj
```

Dynamic libraries: To create dynamic libraries, we slightly modify the files `hellofirst.cpp` and `hellosecond.cpp`, naming the modified files `shellofirst.cpp` and `shellosecond.cpp`, respectively:

```
/* shellofirst.cpp */

#include <iostream>

using namespace std;

void shellofirst(){
    cout << "The first hello from
    ↪ a shared library\n";
}
```

```
/* shellosecond.cpp */

#include <iostream>

using namespace std;

void shellosecond(){
    cout << "The second hello
    ↪ from a shared library\n";
}
```

We will also make the program that calls the functions from these files by analogy, calling it `stwohellos.cpp`:

```
/* stwohellos.cpp */

void shellofirst(void);
void shellosecond(void);

int main(){
  shellofirst();
  shellosecond();

  return(0);
}
```

To compile dynamic-link libraries, the compiler must be given one more instruction to produce relocatable object code, because such libraries can be loaded at different addresses in the address space of the process using the library. The -fpic option is used for this; the abbreviation 'pic' means position independent code:

```
>g++ -c -fpic shellofirst.cpp shellosecond.cpp
```

Finally, to combine the created object files into a dynamic-link library with a .dll extension (under Linux, it is .so), the -shared option must be used, which instructs the linker to create the library file accordingly:

```
>g++ -shared shellofirst.o shellosecond.o -o hello.dll
```

Creating dynamic-link libraries with the Microsoft C/C++ compiler is much more complicated. We have to modify our three *.cpp files to create such a library using the Microsoft compiler, as well as introduce a new helper file hello.h into the game:

```
/* shellofirst.cpp */

#ifdef _MSC_VER
   #define HELLO_EXPORTS
   #include "hello.h"
#endif
#include <iostream>

void shellofirst(){
    std::cout << "The first hello
    ↪ from a shared library\n";
}
```

```
/* shellosecond.cpp */

#ifdef _MSC_VER
   #define HELLO_EXPORTS
   #include "hello.h"
#endif
#include <iostream>

void shellosecond(){
    std::cout << "The second
    ↪ hello from a shared
    ↪ library\n";
}
```

```
/* stwohellos.cpp */        /* hello.h
                               MinGW compiler does not need this file.
#ifdef _MSC_VER             */
  #include "hello.h"
#else                       #pragma once
  void shellofirst(void);
  void shellosecond(void);  #ifdef HELLO_EXPORTS
#endif                        #define HELLO_API __declspec(dllexport)
                            #else
int main(){                   #define HELLO_API __declspec(dllimport)
  shellofirst();            #endif
  shellosecond();
                            extern "C" {
  return 0;                   HELLO_API void shellofirst(void);
}                             HELLO_API void shellosecond(void);
                            }
```

hello.h contains function declarations from dynamic-link libraries for export and import according to the rules of the Microsoft C/C++ compiler.

You can also declare functions like this:

```
extern "C" HELLO_API void shellofirst(void);
extern "C" HELLO_API void shellosecond(void);
```

Note These files can be processed by both MinGW and Microsoft C/C++ compilers. To do this, we have included conditional compilation directives that allow us to automatically determine which compiler is used at the time of compilation: for example, the _MSC_VER constant is defined for the Microsoft C/C ++ compiler.

When compiling with the Microsoft C/C++ compiler, we use option /EHsc to avoid

```
warning C4530: C++ exception handler used, but unwind semantics
↪ are not enabled. Specify /EHsc
```

First, run the command

```
D:\Users\C++\MSVC>cl /EHsc /c shellofirst.cpp shellosecond.cpp
Microsoft (R) C/C++ Optimizing Compiler Version 19.31.31107 for
↪ x64
Copyright (C) Microsoft Corporation. All rights reserved.
```

to compile shellofirst.cpp and shellosecond.cpp to get object files shellofirst.obj and shellosecond.obj, respectively.

Now with the aid of the `lib` utility with the `/DEF` option, we will get `hello.lib` and object `hello.exp`:

```
D:\Users\C++\MSVC>lib /DEF /out:hello.lib shellofirst.obj
↪   shellosecond.obj
Microsoft (R) Library Manager Version 14.31.31107.0
Copyright (C) Microsoft Corporation.  All rights reserved.

   Creating library hello.lib and object hello.exp
```

The `lib` utility with the `/DEF` option creates an import library with a `.lib` extension and an export file with a `.exp` extension. Further, the `link` utility uses the export file to create executable files (usually, a dynamic-link library, dll), and the import library is used to resolve references when creating programs using the created dll.

Finally, the `link` utility with the `/DLL` switch creates the required `hello.dll` library from our object files `shellofirst.obj` and `shellosecond.obj`:

```
D:\Users\C++\MSVC>link /DLL /out:hello.dll shellofirst.obj
↪   shellosecond.obj
Microsoft (R) Incremental Linker Version 14.31.31107.0
Copyright (C) Microsoft Corporation.  All rights reserved.

   Creating library hello.lib and object hello.exp
```

Note that the include file `hello.h` is involved in compilation and build process indirectly: in the files `shellofirst.cpp` and `shellosecond.cpp`, `hello.h` is included through conditional compilation directives:

```
#ifdef _MSC_VER
    #define HELLO_EXPORTS
    #include "hello.h"
#endif
```

Since the `_MSC_VER` constant is just defined when compiling with the Microsoft C/C++ compiler, then through the directive

```
#define HELLO_EXPORTS
```

the `HELLO_EXPORTS` constant will also be defined, which in turn will activate the directive

```
#define HELLO_API __declspec(dllexport)
```

in the contents of the `hello.h` file, being now included in the `shellofirst.cpp` and `shellosecond.cpp` files. Thus, all this will lead to the fact that when compiling the `shellofirst.cpp` and `shellosecond.cpp` files, the function descriptions

```
extern "C" {
    HELLO_API void shellofirst(void);
    HELLO_API void shellosecond(void);
}
```

turn into

```
extern "C" {
    __declspec(dllexport) void shellofirst(void);
    __declspec(dllexport) void shellosecond(void);
}
```

This means that these functions will be exported from the object library. The Microsoft C/C++ compiler directive __declspec(dllexport) serves just to designate exported objects.

Using the dumpbin[5] utility with the /EXPORTS switch, we can check whether the hello.dll library actually exports our functions:

```
D:\Users\C++\MSVC>dumpbin /EXPORTS hello.dll
Microsoft (R) COFF/PE Dumper Version 14.31.31107.0
Copyright (C) Microsoft Corporation.  All rights reserved.


Dump of file hello.dll

File Type: DLL

  Section contains the following exports for hello.dll

    00000000 characteristics
    FFFFFFFF time date stamp
        0.00 version
           1 ordinal base
           2 number of functions
           2 number of names

    ordinal hint RVA      name

          1    0 00001150 shellofirst
          2    1 00003CA0 shellosecond

  Summary

        3000 .data
        3000 .pdata
       12000 .rdata
        1000 .reloc
       23000 .text
        1000 _RDATA
```

---

[5] This utility comes with the Microsoft C/C++ compiler.

10.4   Conclusion

In this chapter, we have shown, using a simple example, the creation of static and dynamic libraries using each of the MinGW and Microsoft C/C++ compilers. In the case of the Microsoft C/C++ compiler, the technical literature mainly describes the creation of libraries using the WinAPI interface. We followed a different, less commonly used method, described in the Microsoft documentation.

Using Libraries

11

In this chapter, we will continue with the example programs of the previous chapter and demonstrate the use of static and dynamic-link libraries, again using the MinGW and Microsoft C/C++ compilers.

11.1 Linking with Static Libraries

The library created in Chapter 10 can now be used in different ways, for example:

```
g++ twohellos.cpp libhello.a -o twohellos
```

In this case, the name of the linked library is written in full, with the path (in our case, the library is in the current directory, so there is no need to provide the path). However, it is common to use the following binding format:

```
g++ twohellos.cpp -lhello -o twohellos -L./
```

In this case, '-lhello' expands to 'libhello.a', and this library is searched for in the directory specified by the '-L' key, that is, in the current directory '. / '. If you omit this switch, the libhello.a library file will not be found! But the slash can be omitted:

```
g++ twohellos.cpp -lhello -o twohellos -L.
```

```
cl twohellos.cpp libhello.lib /link /out:twohellos.exe
```

```
cl twohellos.cpp /link libhello.lib /out:twohellos.exe
```

© The Author(s), under exclusive license to APress Media, LLC,
part of Springer Nature 2024
B. I. Tuleuov, A. B. Ospanova, *Beginning C++ Compilers*,
https://doi.org/10.1007/978-1-4842-9563-2_11

11.2   Linking with Dynamic Libraries

```
D:\Users\C++\MinGW>g++ stwohellos.cpp hello.dll -o stwohellos.exe

D:\Users\C++\MinGW>stwohellos.exe
The first hello from a shared library
The second hello from a shared library

D:\Users\C++\MinGW>

D:\Users\C++\MSVC>cl stwohellos.cpp hello.lib
Microsoft (R) C/C++ Optimizing Compiler Version 19.31.31107 for
↪  x64
Copyright (C) Microsoft Corporation.  All rights reserved.

stwohellos.cpp
Microsoft (R) Incremental Linker Version 14.31.31107.0
Copyright (C) Microsoft Corporation.  All rights reserved.

/out:stwohellos.exe
stwohellos.obj
hello.lib
```

Now again using dumpbin, but with a different /IMPORTS switch, let's
see if our program stwohellos.exe imports our functions exported from the
dynamic-link library hello.dll we built in the previous chapter:

```
C:\User\C++\MSVC>dumpbin /IMPORTS stwohellos.exe
Microsoft (R) COFF/PE Dumper Version 14.31.31107.0
Copyright (C) Microsoft Corporation.  All rights reserved.


Dump of file stwohellos.exe

File Type: EXECUTABLE IMAGE

  Section contains the following imports:

    hello.dll
             140010250 Import Address Table
             140019170 Import Name Table
                     0 time date stamp
                     0 Index of first forwarder reference

                   1 shellosecond
                   0 shellofirst

    KERNEL32.dll
             140010000 Import Address Table
             140018F20 Import Name Table
                     0 time date stamp
                     0 Index of first forwarder reference

                 64A WriteConsoleW
                  94 CloseHandle
                 470 QueryPerformanceCounter
```

```
233 GetCurrentProcessId
237 GetCurrentThreadId
30A GetSystemTimeAsFileTime
38A InitializeSListHead
4F5 RtlCaptureContext
4FD RtlLookupFunctionEntry
504 RtlVirtualUnwind
3A0 IsDebuggerPresent
5E6 UnhandledExceptionFilter
5A4 SetUnhandledExceptionFilter
2F1 GetStartupInfoW
3A8 IsProcessorFeaturePresent
295 GetModuleHandleW
 DA CreateFileW
503 RtlUnwindEx
27D GetLastError
564 SetLastError
149 EnterCriticalSection
3E0 LeaveCriticalSection
123 DeleteCriticalSection
386 InitializeCriticalSectionAndSpinCount
5D6 TlsAlloc
5D8 TlsGetValue
5D9 TlsSetValue
5D7 TlsFree
1C5 FreeLibrary
2CD GetProcAddress
3E6 LoadLibraryExW
145 EncodePointer
487 RaiseException
4FF RtlPcToFileHeader
2F3 GetStdHandle
64B WriteFile
291 GetModuleFileNameW
232 GetCurrentProcess
178 ExitProcess
5C4 TerminateProcess
294 GetModuleHandleExW
1F0 GetCommandLineA
1F1 GetCommandLineW
36C HeapAlloc
370 HeapFree
18F FindClose
195 FindFirstFileExW
1A6 FindNextFileW
3AE IsValidCodePage
1CC GetACP
2B6 GetOEMCP
1DB GetCPInfo
412 MultiByteToWideChar
637 WideCharToMultiByte
253 GetEnvironmentStringsW
1C4 FreeEnvironmentStringsW
546 SetEnvironmentVariableW
57F SetStdHandle
26A GetFileType
2F8 GetStringTypeW
1B4 FlsAlloc
```

```
                                      1B6  FlsGetValue
                                      1B7  FlsSetValue
                                      1B5  FlsFree
                                       AA  CompareStringW
                                      3D4  LCMapStringW
                                      2D4  GetProcessHeap
                                      375  HeapSize
                                      373  HeapReAlloc
                                      1B9  FlushFileBuffers
                                      21A  GetConsoleOutputCP
                                      216  GetConsoleMode
                                      555  SetFilePointerEx

     Summary

              2000  .data
              2000  .pdata
              A000  .rdata
              1000  .reloc
              F000  .text
              1000  _RDATA


D:\Users\C++\MSVC>stwohellos.exe
The first hello from a shared library
The second hello from a shared library

C:\User\C++\MSVC>
```

11.3   Using Libraries from Source Code

Naturally, the program can be built directly without creating the `libhello.a` library:

```
g++ twohellos.cpp hellofirst.cpp hellosecond.cpp -o twohellos
```

but, in general, it does not make sense to compile `hellofirst.cpp` and `hellosecond.cpp` auxiliary files every time the main `twohellos.cpp` file is compiled:

```
cl twohellos.cpp hellofirst.cpp hellosecond.cpp /link
↪   /out:twohellos.exe

C:\User\C++>twohellos.exe
The first hello
The second hello

C:\User\C++>
```

As an illustrative example, here is an example of an Assembler program that uses an I/O library written in C++. Recall that the Assembly language does not have a standard library, but under Windows in this language, you can use the C standard library or calls to WinAPI functions. The latter provides more options on Windows;

however, the amount of code in this case is significantly larger. In simple cases and in the case of scientific computing, this is true; standard C library functions (such as `printf`) are sufficient, and the code size remains quite moderate. The book on 64-bit Assembly Programming [30] provides many examples of programs that use I/O functions from the C standard library, called through a C++ helper program. The build of the program takes place in two stages: each program is compiled separately, then the object modules are linked to create an executable file. We will do this: we will remove all unnecessary data from the auxiliary C++ file and build a static library from it, which we will link with the object module obtained as a result of compiling the program in the Assembly language.

Let's take the code from Listing 2–3 [30, page 64] as the Assembly language program. In the `listing2-3.asm` program, we make minimal changes: before the line

```
option casemap:none
```

insert the following three lines:

```
includelib msvcrt.lib
includelib legacy_stdio_definitions.lib
includelibMyLibrary.lib
```

and all occurrences of the function name `'asmMain'` should be replaced by `'main'` (there are only three such occurrences).

In the `c.cpp` helper program (Listing 1–7 [30, page 28]), remove the line

```
void asmMain(void);
```

and completely remove the `int main(void)` function, since the library does not need it. Save the modified file as `MyLibrary.cpp`. The texts of the modified programs are given as follows:

```
//
// MyLibrary.cpp
// compile with: cl /c /EHsc MyLibrary.cpp
// post-build command: lib MyLibrary.obj
//
//
// Generic C++ driver program to demonstrate returning function
// results from assembly language to C++. Also includes a
// "readLine" function that reads a string from the user and
// passes it on to the assembly language code.
//
// Need to include stdio.h so this program can call "printf"
// and stdio.h so this program can call strlen.

#include <errno.h>
#include <stdio.h>
#include <stdlib.h>
#include <string.h>

// extern "C" namespace prevents "name mangling" by the C++
```

```
// compiler.

extern "C" {
    // getTitle returns a pointer to a string of characters
// from the assembly code that specifies the title of that
// program (that makes this program generic and usable
    // with a large number of sample programs in "The Art of
// 64-bit Assembly Language."

    char *getTitle(void);

    // C++ function that the assembly
    // language program can call:

    int readLine(char *dest, int maxLen);

};

// readLine reads a line of text from the user (from the
// console device) and stores that string into the destination
// buffer the first argument specifies. Strings are limited in
// length to the value specified by the second argument
// (minus 1).
//
// This function returns the number of characters actually
// read, or -1 if there was an error.
//
// Note that if the user enters too many characters (maxlen or
// more) then this function only returns the first maxlen-1
// characters. This is not considered an error.

int readLine(char *dest, int maxLen){
    // Note: fgets returns NULL if there was an error, else
// it returns a pointer to the string data read (which
// will be the value of the dest pointer).

    char *result = fgets(dest, maxLen, stdin);
    if (result != NULL){
        // Wipe out the new line character at the
        // end of the string:

        int len = strlen(result);
        if (len > 0){
            dest[len - 1] = 0;
        }
        return len;
    }
    return -1; // If there was an error.
}
```

Here' the slightly modified listing of the program `listing2-3.asm`:

```
; Listing 2-3
;
; Demonstrate two's complement operation and input of numeric
↪  values.
; msvcrt.lib(initializers.obj) : warning LNK4098: defaultlib
↪  'libcmt.lib' conflicts with use of other libs; use
↪  /NODEFAULTLIB:library
; ml64 listing2-3.asm /link /NODEFAULTLIB:libcmt.lib
        includelib msvcrt.lib
        includelib legacy_stdio_definitions.lib
        includelib MyLibrary.lib

        option  casemap:none

nl      =       10  ;ASCII code for newline
maxLen  =       256

        .data
titleStr byte    'Listing 2-3', 0

prompt1  byte    "Enter an integer between 0 and 127: ", 0
fmtStr1  byte    "Value in hexadecimal: %x", nl, 0
fmtStr2  byte    "Invert all the bits (hexadecimal): %x", nl, 0
fmtStr3  byte    "Add 1 (hexadecimal): %x", nl, 0
fmtStr4  byte    "Output as signed integer: %d", nl, 0
fmtStr5  byte    "Using neg instruction: %d", nl, 0

intValue sqword ?
input    byte    maxLen dup (?)


        .code
        externdef printf:proc
        externdef atoi:proc
        externdef readLine:proc

; Return program title to C++ program:

        public getTitle
getTitle proc
        lea rax, titleStr
        ret
getTitle endp


; Here is the "main" function.


        public  main
main     proc
```

```
; "Magic" instruction offered without explanation at this point:

            sub     rsp, 56

; Read an unsigned integer from the user: This code will blindly
; assume that the user's input was correct. The atoi function
↪  returns
; zero if there was some sort of error on the user input. Later
; chapters in Ao64A will describe how to check for errors from
↪  the
; user.

            lea     rcx, prompt1
            call    printf

            lea     rcx, input
            mov     rdx, maxLen
            call    readLine

; Call C stdlib atoi function.
;
; i = atoi( str )

            lea     rcx, input
            call    atoi
;           and     rax, 0ffh ; Only keep L.O. eight bits
            mov     intValue, rax

; Print the input value (in decimal) as a hexadecimal number:

            lea     rcx, fmtStr1
            mov     rdx, rax
            call    printf

; Perform the two's complement operation on the input number.
; Begin by inverting all the bits (just work with a byte here).

            mov     rdx, intValue
            not     dl        ;Only work with 8-bit values!
            lea     rcx, fmtStr2
            call    printf

; Invert all the bits and add 1 (still working with just a byte)

            mov     rdx, intValue
            not     rdx
            add     rdx, 1
            and     rdx, 0ffh ; Only keep L.O. eight bits
            lea     rcx, fmtStr3
            call    printf

; Negate the value and print as a signed integer (work with a
↪  full
```

```
; integer here, because C++ %d format specifier expects a 32-bit
; integer. H.O. 32 bits of RDX get ignored by C++.

                mov        rdx, intValue
                not        rdx
                add        rdx, 1
                lea        rcx, fmtStr4
                call       printf
```

; Negate the value using the neg instruction.

```
                mov        rdx, intValue
                neg        rdx
                lea        rcx, fmtStr5
                call       printf
```

; Another "magic" instruction that undoes the effect of the
↪ previous
; one before this procedure returns to its caller.

```
                add        rsp, 56
                ret        ;Returns to caller
main            endp
                end
```

Compiling `MyLibrary.cpp` and building the `MyLibrary.lib` library

```
>cl /c /EHsc MyLibrary.cpp
>lib MyLibrary.obj
```

Compiling the assembly program and linking the object file with the static library `MyLibrary.lib`

```
>ml64 listing2-3.asm /link /NODEFAULTLIB:libcmt.lib
```

The linker parameter `/NODEFAULTLIB:libcmt.lib` is needed to fix the warning:

```
msvcrt.lib(initializers.obj) : warning LNK4098: defaultlib
↪  'libcmt.lib' conflicts with use of other libs; use
↪  /NODEFAULTLIB:library
```

Here's the result of the program call:

```
C:\User\C++\Book>listing2-3.exe
Enter an integer between 0 and 127: 117
Value in hexadecimal: 75
Invert all the bits (hexadecimal): 8a
Add 1 (hexadecimal): 8b
Output as signed integer: -117
Using neg instruction: -117

C:\User\C++\Book>
```

11.4   Universal CRT Deployment

As already noted, the C/C++ runtime libraries are part of these languages, and each implementation of these languages tends to create its own implementation of these libraries as well. The standard implementation of the C language for older versions (starting from 4.2 to 6.0 from Visual Studio 98) of the Microsoft C/C++ compiler was called MSVCRT.DLL. Although this library is old, it is still included to make old programs run. The corresponding C++ library was named MSVCP*.DLL (the asterisk denotes the version number of the library).

Library versions before 4.0 and 7.0–13.0 were already marked as MSVCR*. DLL, again with the library version number instead of an asterisk.

In the future, with each new version of the compiler, the runtime library was also updated, indicated by the corresponding number. Along with Visual Studio, Microsoft also distributed these libraries separately under the name Visual C++ Redistributable Libraries. These libraries are located in the C:\Windows\System32 folder.

By now, there are so many versions of these libraries that it already creates certain problems. If the user has many applications installed on the machine, then there may be many such libraries. Starting with compiler version 12.0 (Visual Studio 2013), each major version of the compiler included its own runtime library, for example, for version 11 (Visual Studio 2012) it is msvcr110.dll, and for version 12 (Visual Studio 2013) it is msvcr120.dll. By the time compiler version 14.0 was released, most of the C/C++ libraries had already been merged into a new DLL called UCRTBASE.DLL. In fact, when linking from this DLL, calls were redirected to another new DLL called VCRuntime*.DLL (VCRUNTIME140.DLL).

So the situation has changed since compiler version 14 (Visual Studio 2015). This and subsequent versions of the compiler already use the aforementioned one library, the so-called universal, which is now part of the operating system: this library is now included in Windows 10 and above and Windows Server 2016 and above. The Universal CRT (UCRT) is a Microsoft Windows operating system component.

Thus, Visual C++ C Runtime (CRT) now consists of two parts: VCRuntime and Universal CRT. VCRuntime contains components responsible for starting processes and handling exceptions, and UCRT is, as it were, an analog of GNU glibc from Linux for Windows; this part of the library contains the standard part of the C runtime library that includes POSIX functionality.

This UCRT library can also be installed on older versions of Windows that still have extended support through Windows Update.

Manual installation of this library (so-called local deployment) is also supported, with some limitations; however, Microsoft does not recommend this for security and performance reasons.

The DLLs for local deployment are also included in the Windows SDK; they are located in the directory:

```
C:\Program Files (x86)\Windows
↪   Kits\10\Redist\%Version%\ucrt\DLLs\%ARCH%
```

where %ARCH% means computer architecture. The set of DLLs required for deployment consists, in addition to ucrtbase.dll, also of the so-called APISet forwarder DLLs under the name api-ms-win-*.dll. For local deployment, it is highly recommended to include all of these DLLs, although the APISet forwarder DLLs may differ for each operating system.

Two important notes about local deployment: Since the Universal CRT is a component of the core operating system component starting from Windows 10 and later, it is the Universal CRT from the system directory that will be used, even if there is a more recent version of the Universal CRT library in the local application directory.

On versions of Windows prior to Windows 8 (Windows before Windows 8), Universal CRTs cannot be used unless they are located in the same directory as the application that uses them, because in this case APISet forwarder DLLs are unable to resolve the ucrtbase.dll successfully.

Naturally, with static linking to the Universal CRT, there will be no such problem. You can also deploy this library centrally through Windows Update and finally place the library files in the application folder.

Deployment on Microsoft Windows XP: As you know, Visual Studio 2015 and Visual Studio 2017 support development for the Microsoft Windows XP operating system. The Universal CRT can also be deployed on Microsoft Windows XP. Since Microsoft Windows XP is no longer officially supported, the deployment of the Universal CRT onto Microsoft Windows XP is different than the standard process. When installing the corresponding Visual C++ Redistributable on Windows XP, the installer directly installs the Universal CRT and related files in the system directory without using Windows Update. The same applies to Microsoft_VC<version>_CRT_<target>.msm files and the Redistributable merge modules.

Universal CRT local deployment on Windows XP is carried out in the same way as described earlier.

Here is a quote from the Microsoft website [27]:

Note Runtime library support for Windows XP is no longer available in the latest Visual C++ Redistributable for Visual Studio 2015, 2017, 2019 and 2022. The last redistributable to support Windows XP is version 16.7 (file version 14.27.29114.0). If your Windows XP apps are deployed with or updated to a later version of the redistributable, the apps won't run. For more information, and how to get a version of the redistributable that supports Windows XP, see Configuring programs for Windows XP [28].

11.5   Conclusion

This chapter is directly related to the previous one, as here we have shown the use of the libraries created in the previous chapter. We also demonstrated the use of libraries by directly including their source code in the application.

We also touched on the use of the relatively new runtime library Windows Universal CRT (UCRT).

GMP (GNU Multiprecision Library)

12

GNU Multiprecision Library (GMP) is a free arbitrary-precision arithmetic library for working with signed integers, rationals, and floating-point numbers. In practice, the accuracy is limited only by the available memory on the computer where this library is used.

It has a rich feature set with an intuitive interface, mainly used in cryptographic applications and research, Internet-related applications, computer algebra systems (symbol manipulation), and computational algebra research.

The library has been carefully designed to provide maximum performance for both small and large operands. This is achieved by using full words as the basic arithmetic type, fast algorithms, and highly optimized assembler codes for the most common types of inner loops for many types of processors.

GMP is constantly updated and maintained. New issues appear at intervals of about a year. Its official site is http://gmplib.org. A very detailed online help can be found at [31]. The current version at the time of this writing is 6.2.1 (March 2023).

The library is intended mainly for Unix-like systems such as GNU/Linux, Solaris, HP-UX, Mac OS X/Darwin, BSD, AIX, etc. It also works on Windows systems in both 32-bit and 64-bit modes.

Starting with version 6, GMP is distributed under a dual license: GNU LGPL v3 and GNU GPL v2. This means that the library can be freely used, distributed, and improved, as well as transferred to third parties, binary codes linked with this library. Restrictions apply only when used in conjunction with proprietary programs. One of the best computer algebra systems (math packages), Maple, by Waterloo Maple Inc., uses GMP for integer long arithmetic (www.maplesoft.com/support/help/Maple/view.aspx?path=copyright, www.maplesoft.com/support/downloads/GMP.html).

The library includes several categories of functions:

1. High-level arithmetic functions for working with signed integers, starting with the prefix `mpz_`: There are about 150 of them. The corresponding type is `mpz_t`.

B. I. Tuleuov, A. B. Ospanova, *Beginning C++ Compilers*, https://doi.org/10.1007/978-1-4842-9563-2_12

2. High-level rational arithmetic functions starting with the `mpq_` prefix: The corresponding type is `mpq_t`. There are about 35 such functions, but signed integer arithmetic functions can also be used separately in the numerator and denominator.

3. High-level floating-point arithmetic functions starting with the `mpf_` prefix: The corresponding type is `mpf_t`. This category includes about 70 functions. This category of GMP functions should be used if the standard C/C++ `double` type precision is not sufficient. It is highly recommended for new projects to use the MPFR library, which is an essential extension of GMP toward `mpf`.

4. C++ class-based interface for all of the preceding function categories: Naturally, functions and types in C can be used directly from C++.

5. Fast low-level functions for working with natural numbers, starting with the prefix `mpn_`: The corresponding type is an array of values like `mp_limb_t`. These functions are used by the functions of the previous categories, but they can also be used directly in time-critical user applications. They are not so easy to use; memory management is not implemented—the side calling these functions itself must take care of allocating sufficient memory for the returned values. Such functions take input arguments as a pair consisting of a pointer to the least significant word and an integer indicating how many words the argument consists of (its size). There are about 60 functions in this category.

6. Various auxiliary functions: Functions for preparing the workspace, for generating random numbers.

The functions of the GMP library, with some exceptions, have the reentrant property and are thread-safe, which allows it to be used in multithreaded (parallel) applications. For details, please refer to section 3.7 of the user manual for this library.

12.1   Building

Since the library actively uses assembler inserts for the most critical operations in terms of efficiency, the GMP library should be compiled on the target (i.e., where it is intended to be used) machine to achieve the best performance, since the assembly language is highly dependent on the specific platform. In particular, building and running the `tuneup` utility from the `tune` directory can be very useful for applications that take a long time to run or use extremely large numbers. For example, the command sequence

```
cd tune
make tuneup
./tuneup
```

generates a parameter header file `gmp-mparam.h` that is more specific to the local machine. After that, the library code must be recompiled. `tuneup` has one useful option `'-f NNN'` which can be used when dealing with extremely large numbers, in which case tuneup should be run with a large NNN value.

Under Windows, GMP can be built using several ports of GCC and the GNU build tools. These are Cygwin, DJGPP, and MinGW. We do not consider Cygwin due to its massiveness and extra layer, and DJGPP is too outdated, as it only supports MS-DOS and 32-bit Windows.

Build with MinGW

```
E:\Users>mingw81

E:\Users>set PATH=E:\Programs\msys\bin;%PATH%
```

or

```
E:\Users>msys[.bat]

E:\Users>bash

bash-3.1$ cd G:\Users

bash-3.1$ ls
gmp-6.2.1.tar.xz
```

Unpack the archive gmp-6.2.1.tar.xz and change to newly created directory gmp-6.2.1:

```
bash-3.1$ tar xJf gmp-6.2.1.tar.xz && cd gmp-6.2.1
```

Now run the configure script with the `'--enable-cxx'` option in order to support the C++ interface:

```
bash-3.1$ ./configure --enable-cxx
. . .
configure: summary of build options:

    Version:           GNU MP 6.2.1
    Host type:         nehalem-pc-mingw32
    ABI:               64
    Install prefix:    /usr/local
    Compiler:          gcc
    Static libraries:  yes
    Shared libraries:  no
```

Now it is time to launch the build process:

```
bash-3.1$ make
```

After the successful completion of the build process, the GMP developers strongly recommend that you run the command

```
bash-3.1$ make check
```

If that fails, or you care about the performance of GMP, you need to read the full instructions in the chapter "Installing GMP" in the manual.

You should not skip the "make check" part; the risk that the GMP sources are miscompiled is unfortunately quite high. And if they indeed are, "make check" is very likely to trigger the compiler-introduced bug.

```
.  .  .
make   check-TESTS
make[4]: Entering directory `/g/Users/gmp-6.2.1/tests'
make[5]: Entering directory `/g/Users/gmp-6.2.1/tests'
PASS: t-bswap.exe          PASS: t-modlinv.exe
PASS: t-constants.exe      PASS: t-popc.exe
PASS: t-count_zeros.exe    PASS: t-parity.exe
PASS: t-hightomask.exe     PASS: t-sub.exe
==================================================================
Testsuite summary for GNU MP 6.2.1
==================================================================
# TOTAL: 8
# PASS:  8
# SKIP:  0
# XFAIL: 0
# FAIL:  0
# XPASS: 0
# ERROR: 0
==================================================================
    .  .  .

make   check-TESTS
make[4]: Entering directory `/g/Users/gmp-6.2.1/tests/mpn'
make[5]: Entering directory `/g/Users/gmp-6.2.1/tests/mpn'
PASS: t-asmtype.exe        PASS: t-toom2-sqr.exe
PASS: t-aors_1.exe         PASS: t-toom3-sqr.exe
PASS: t-divrem_1.exe       PASS: t-toom4-sqr.exe
PASS: t-mod_1.exe          PASS: t-toom6-sqr.exe
PASS: t-fat.exe            PASS: t-toom8-sqr.exe
PASS: t-get_d.exe          PASS: t-div.exe
PASS: t-instrument.exe     PASS: t-mul.exe
PASS: t-iord_u.exe         PASS: t-mullo.exe
PASS: t-mp_bases.exe       PASS: t-sqrlo.exe
PASS: t-perfsqr.exe        PASS: t-mulmod_bnm1.exe
PASS: t-scan.exe           PASS: t-sqrmod_bnm1.exe
PASS: logic.exe            PASS: t-mulmid.exe
PASS: t-toom22.exe         PASS: t-hgcd.exe
PASS: t-toom32.exe         PASS: t-hgcd_appr.exe
PASS: t-toom33.exe         PASS: t-matrix22.exe
PASS: t-toom42.exe         PASS: t-invert.exe
PASS: t-toom43.exe         PASS: t-bdiv.exe
PASS: t-toom44.exe         PASS: t-fib2m.exe
PASS: t-toom52.exe         PASS: t-broot.exe
PASS: t-toom53.exe         PASS: t-brootinv.exe
PASS: t-toom54.exe         PASS: t-minvert.exe
PASS: t-toom62.exe         PASS: t-sizeinbase.exe
```

```
PASS: t-toom63.exe          PASS: t-gcd_11.exe
PASS: t-toom6h.exe          PASS: t-gcd_22.exe
PASS: t-toom8h.exe          PASS: t-gcdext_1.exe
==================================================================
Testsuite summary for GNU MP 6.2.1
==================================================================
# TOTAL: 50
# PASS:  50
# SKIP:  0
# XFAIL: 0
# FAIL:  0
# XPASS: 0
# ERROR: 0
==================================================================
. . .

make   check-TESTS
make[4]: Entering directory `/g/Users/gmp-6.2.1/tests/mpz'
make[5]: Entering directory `/g/Users/gmp-6.2.1/tests/mpz'
PASS: reuse.exe             PASS: t-get_d_2exp.exe
PASS: t-addsub.exe          PASS: t-get_si.exe
PASS: t-cmp.exe             PASS: t-set_d.exe
PASS: t-mul.exe             PASS: t-set_si.exe
PASS: t-mul_i.exe           PASS: t-lucm.exe
PASS: t-tdiv.exe            PASS: t-fac_ui.exe
PASS: t-tdiv_ui.exe         PASS: t-mfac_uiui.exe
PASS: t-fdiv.exe            PASS: t-primorial_ui.exe
PASS: t-fdiv_ui.exe         PASS: t-fib_ui.exe
PASS: t-cdiv_ui.exe         PASS: t-lucnum_ui.exe
PASS: t-gcd.exe             PASS: t-scan.exe
PASS: t-gcd_ui.exe          PASS: t-fits.exe
PASS: t-lcm.exe             PASS: t-divis.exe
PASS: t-invert.exe          PASS: t-divis_2exp.exe
PASS: dive.exe              PASS: t-cong.exe
PASS: dive_ui.exe           PASS: t-cong_2exp.exe
PASS: t-sqrtrem.exe         PASS: t-sizeinbase.exe
PASS: convert.exe           PASS: t-set_str.exe
PASS: io.exe                PASS: t-aorsmul.exe
PASS: t-inp_str.exe         PASS: t-cmp_d.exe
PASS: logic.exe             PASS: t-cmp_si.exe
PASS: t-bit.exe             PASS: t-hamdist.exe
PASS: t-powm.exe            PASS: t-oddeven.exe
PASS: t-powm_ui.exe         PASS: t-popcount.exe
PASS: t-pow.exe             PASS: t-set_f.exe
PASS: t-div_2exp.exe        PASS: t-io_raw.exe
PASS: t-root.exe            PASS: t-import.exe
PASS: t-perfsqr.exe         PASS: t-export.exe
PASS: t-perfpow.exe         PASS: t-pprime_p.exe
PASS: t-jac.exe             PASS: t-nextprime.exe
PASS: t-bin.exe             PASS: t-remove.exe
PASS: t-get_d.exe           PASS: t-limbs.exe
==================================================================
Testsuite summary for GNU MP 6.2.1
```

```
=================================================================
# TOTAL: 64
# PASS:  64
# SKIP:  0
# XFAIL: 0
# FAIL:  0
# XPASS: 0
# ERROR: 0
=================================================================
. . .

make   check-TESTS
make[4]: Entering directory `/g/Users/gmp-6.2.1/tests/mpq'
make[5]: Entering directory `/g/Users/gmp-6.2.1/tests/mpq'
PASS: t-aors.exe        PASS: t-inv.exe
PASS: t-cmp.exe         PASS: t-md_2exp.exe
PASS: t-cmp_ui.exe      PASS: t-set_f.exe
PASS: t-cmp_si.exe      PASS: t-set_str.exe
PASS: t-equal.exe       PASS: io.exe
PASS: t-get_d.exe       PASS: reuse.exe
PASS: t-get_str.exe     PASS: t-cmp_z.exe
PASS: t-inp_str.exe
=================================================================
Testsuite summary for GNU MP 6.2.1
=================================================================
# TOTAL: 15
# PASS:  15
# SKIP:  0
# XFAIL: 0
# FAIL:  0
# XPASS: 0
# ERROR: 0
=================================================================
. . .

make   check-TESTS
make[4]: Entering directory `/g/Users/gmp-6.2.1/tests/mpf'
make[5]: Entering directory `/g/Users/gmp-6.2.1/tests/mpf'
PASS: t-dm2exp.exe        PASS: t-get_si.exe
PASS: t-conv.exe          PASS: t-get_ui.exe
PASS: t-add.exe           PASS: t-gsprec.exe
PASS: t-sub.exe           PASS: t-inp_str.exe
PASS: t-sqrt.exe          PASS: t-int_p.exe
PASS: t-sqrt_ui.exe       PASS: t-mul_ui.exe
PASS: t-muldiv.exe        PASS: t-set.exe
PASS: reuse.exe           PASS: t-set_q.exe
PASS: t-cmp_d.exe         PASS: t-set_si.exe
PASS: t-cmp_si.exe        PASS: t-set_ui.exe
PASS: t-div.exe           PASS: t-trunc.exe
PASS: t-fits.exe          PASS: t-ui_div.exe
PASS: t-get_d.exe         PASS: t-eq.exe
PASS: t-get_d_2exp.exe    PASS: t-pow_ui.exe
=================================================================
```

```
Testsuite summary for GNU MP 6.2.1
=====================================================================
# TOTAL: 28
# PASS:  28
# SKIP:  0
# XFAIL: 0
# FAIL:  0
# XPASS: 0
# ERROR: 0
=====================================================================
. . .

make   check-TESTS
make[4]: Entering directory `/g/Users/gmp-6.2.1/tests/rand'
make[5]: Entering directory `/g/Users/gmp-6.2.1/tests/rand'
PASS: t-iset.exe      PASS: t-urbui.exe
PASS: t-lc2exp.exe    PASS: t-urmui.exe
PASS: t-mt.exe        PASS: t-urndmm.exe
PASS: t-rand.exe
=====================================================================
Testsuite summary for GNU MP 6.2.1
=====================================================================
# TOTAL: 7
# PASS:  7
# SKIP:  0
# XFAIL: 0
# FAIL:  0
# XPASS: 0
# ERROR: 0
=====================================================================
. . .

make   check-TESTS
make[4]: Entering directory `/g/Users/gmp-6.2.1/tests/misc'
make[5]: Entering directory `/g/Users/gmp-6.2.1/tests/misc'
PASS: t-printf.exe
PASS: t-scanf.exe
PASS: t-locale.exe
=====================================================================
Testsuite summary for GNU MP 6.2.1
=====================================================================
# TOTAL: 3
# PASS:  3
# SKIP:  0
# XFAIL: 0
# FAIL:  0
# XPASS: 0
# ERROR: 0
=====================================================================
. . .

make   check-TESTS
make[4]: Entering directory `/g/Users/gmp-6.2.1/tests/cxx'
```

```
make[5]: Entering directory `/g/Users/gmp-6.2.1/tests/cxx'
PASS: t-binary.exe      PASS: t-ops2f.exe
PASS: t-cast.exe        PASS: t-ops3.exe
PASS: t-cxx11.exe       PASS: t-ostream.exe
PASS: t-headers.exe     PASS: t-prec.exe
PASS: t-iostream.exe    PASS: t-ternary.exe
PASS: t-istream.exe     PASS: t-unary.exe
PASS: t-locale.exe      PASS: t-ops2z.exe
PASS: t-misc.exe        PASS: t-assign.exe
PASS: t-mix.exe         PASS: t-constr.exe
PASS: t-ops.exe         PASS: t-rand.exe
PASS: t-ops2qf.exe
PASS: t-do-exceptions-work-at-all-with-this-compiler.exe
============================================================
Testsuite summary for GNU MP 6.2.1
============================================================
# TOTAL: 22
# PASS:  22
# SKIP:  0
# XFAIL: 0
# FAIL:  0
# XPASS: 0
# ERROR: 0
============================================================
```

Finally, install the built library:

```
bash-3.1$ make install

. . .
make[2]: Entering directory `/g/Users/gmp-6.2.1'
make[3]: Entering directory `/g/Users/gmp-6.2.1'
 /usr/bin/mkdir -p '/usr/local/lib'
 /bin/sh ./libtool    --mode=install /usr/bin/install -c
 ↪  libgmp.la libgmpxx.la '/usr/local/lib'
libtool: install: /usr/bin/install -c .libs/libgmp.lai
 ↪  /usr/local/lib/libgmp.la
libtool: install: /usr/bin/install -c .libs/libgmpxx.lai
 ↪  /usr/local/lib/libgmpxx.la
libtool: install: /usr/bin/install -c .libs/libgmp.a
 ↪  /usr/local/lib/libgmp.a
libtool: install: chmod 644 /usr/local/lib/libgmp.a
libtool: install: ranlib /usr/local/lib/libgmp.a
libtool: install: /usr/bin/install -c .libs/libgmpxx.a
 ↪  /usr/local/lib/libgmpxx.a
libtool: install: chmod 644 /usr/local/lib/libgmpxx.a
libtool: install: ranlib /usr/local/lib/libgmpxx.a
 /usr/bin/mkdir -p '/usr/local/include'
 /usr/bin/install -c -m 644 gmp.h '/usr/local/include'
 /usr/bin/mkdir -p '/usr/local/include'
 /usr/bin/install -c -m 644 gmpxx.h '/usr/local/include'
 /usr/bin/mkdir -p '/usr/local/lib/pkgconfig'
 /usr/bin/install -c -m 644 gmp.pc gmpxx.pc
 ↪  '/usr/local/lib/pkgconfig'
```

```
make   install-data-hook
make[4]: Entering directory `/g/Users/gmp-6.2.1'

+-----------------------------------------------------------------+
| CAUTION:                                                        |
|                                                                 |
| If you have not already run "make check", then we strongly      |
| recommend you do so.                                            |
|                                                                 |
| GMP has been carefully tested by its authors, but compilers     |
| are all too often released with serious bugs.  GMP tends to     |
| explore interesting corners in compilers and has hit bugs       |
| on quite a few occasions.                                       |
|                                                                 |
+-----------------------------------------------------------------+

make[4]: Leaving directory `/g/Users/gmp-6.2.1'
make[3]: Leaving directory `/g/Users/gmp-6.2.1'
make[2]: Leaving directory `/g/Users/gmp-6.2.1'
make[1]: Leaving directory `/g/Users/gmp-6.2.1'
bash-3.1$
```

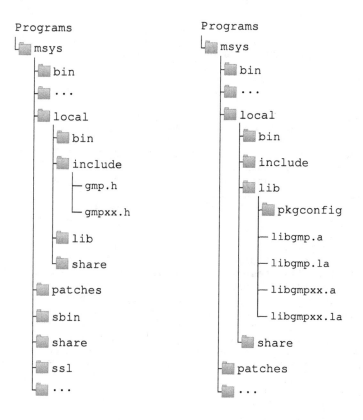

On Windows, by default, GMP can only be built as a static library, but a DLL can be built by running the configure script with the following options:

```
./configure --disable-static --enable-shared
```

That is, the Windows static and dynamic-link libraries cannot be built at the same time because some of the export directives in the gmp.h header file must be different.

Now let's show how to build GMP as a dynamic-link library:

```
./configure --enable-cxx --disable-static --enable-shared
. . .
configure: summary of build options:

  Version:              GNU MP 6.2.1
  Host type:            nehalem-pc-mingw32
  ABI:                  64
  Install prefix:       /usr/local
  Compiler:             gcc
  Static libraries:     no
  Shared libraries:     yes

bash-3.1$
```

Finally, install the built DLL library:

```
bash-3.1$ make install

. . .
make[2]: Entering directory `/g/Users/gmp-6.2.1'
make[3]: Entering directory `/g/Users/gmp-6.2.1'
 /usr/bin/mkdir -p '/usr/local/lib'
 /bin/sh ./libtool   --mode=install /usr/bin/install -c
 ↪  libgmp.la libgmpxx.la '/usr/local/lib'
libtool: install: /usr/bin/install -c .libs/libgmp.dll.a
↪  /usr/local/lib/libgmp.dll.a
libtool: install: base_file=`basename libgmp.la`
libtool: install:  dlpath=`/bin/sh 2>&1 -c '. .libs/'libgmp.la'i;
↪  echo libgmp-10.dll'`
libtool: install:  dldir=/usr/local/lib/`dirname
↪  ../bin/libgmp-10.dll`
libtool: install:  test -d /usr/local/lib/../bin || mkdir -p
↪  /usr/local/lib/../bin
libtool: install:  /usr/bin/install -c .libs/libgmp-10.dll
↪  /usr/local/lib/../bin/libgmp-10.dll
libtool: install:  chmod a+x /usr/local/lib/../bin/libgmp-10.dll
libtool: install:  if test -n '' && test -n 'strip
↪  --strip-unneeded'; then eval 'strip --strip-unneeded
↪  /usr/local/lib/../bin/libgmp-10.dll' || exit 0; fi
libtool: install: /usr/bin/install -c .libs/libgmp.lai
↪  /usr/local/lib/libgmp.la
libtool: install: /usr/bin/install -c .libs/libgmpxx.dll.a
↪  /usr/local/lib/libgmpxx.dll.a
```

```
libtool: install: base_file=`basename libgmpxx.la`
libtool: install:  dlpath=`/bin/sh 2>&1 -c '.
↪    .libs/'libgmpxx.la'i; echo libgmpxx-4.dll'`
libtool: install:  dldir=/usr/local/lib/`dirname
↪    ../bin/libgmpxx-4.dll`
libtool: install:  test -d /usr/local/lib/../bin || mkdir -p
↪    /usr/local/lib/../bin
libtool: install:  /usr/bin/install -c .libs/libgmpxx-4.dll
↪    /usr/local/lib/../bin/libgmpxx-4.dll
libtool: install:  chmod a+x /usr/local/lib/../bin/libgmpxx-4.dll
libtool: install:  if test -n '' && test -n 'strip
↪    --strip-unneeded'; then eval 'strip --strip-unneeded
↪    /usr/local/lib/../bin/libgmpxx-4.dll' || exit 0; fi
libtool: install: /usr/bin/install -c .libs/libgmpxx.lai
↪    /usr/local/lib/libgmpxx.la
 /usr/bin/mkdir -p '/usr/local/include'
 /usr/bin/install -c -m 644 gmp.h '/usr/local/include'
 /usr/bin/mkdir -p '/usr/local/include'
 /usr/bin/install -c -m 644 gmpxx.h '/usr/local/include'
 /usr/bin/mkdir -p '/usr/local/lib/pkgconfig'
 /usr/bin/install -c -m 644 gmp.pc gmpxx.pc
↪    '/usr/local/lib/pkgconfig'
make  install-data-hook
make[4]: Entering directory `/g/Users/gmp-6.2.1'

+---------------------------------------------------------------+
| CAUTION:                                                      |
|                                                              |
| If you have not already run "make check", then we strongly   |
| recommend you do so.                                         |
|                                                              |
| GMP has been carefully tested by its authors, but compilers  |
| are all too often released with serious bugs.  GMP tends to  |
| explore interesting corners in compilers and has hit bugs    |
| on quite a few occasions.                                    |
|                                                              |
+---------------------------------------------------------------+

make[4]: Leaving directory `/g/Users/gmp-6.2.1'
make[3]: Leaving directory `/g/Users/gmp-6.2.1'
make[2]: Leaving directory `/g/Users/gmp-6.2.1'
make[1]: Leaving directory `/g/Users/gmp-6.2.1'
bash-3.1$
```

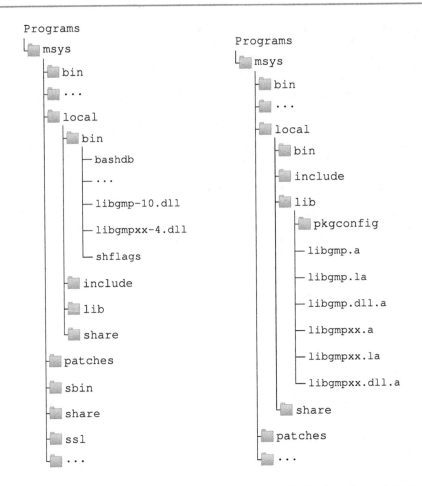

A DLL compiled by the MinGW compiler can be used with the Microsoft C/C++ compiler. The Libtool library tool does not create a .lib format library, but it can be created using Microsoft's lib tool:

```
cd .libs
lib /def:libgmp-3.dll.def /out:libgmp-3.lib
```

You can do the same with libgmpxx.

Run the command line and initialize the Microsoft C/C++ compiler:

```
C:\Users\User>vc 64
*******************************************************************
** Visual Studio 2022 Developer Command Prompt v17.1.5
** Copyright (c) 2022 Microsoft Corporation
*******************************************************************
[vcvarsall.bat] Environment initialized for: 'x64'
```

Change to the `gmp-6.2.1\.libs` subdirectory where the object files that make up the dynamic-link library are located:

```
C:\Users\User>cd /d G:\Users\gmp-6.2.1\.libs

G:\Users\gmp-6.2.1\.libs>
```

Let's look at the contents of this directory:

```
G:\Users\gmp-6.2.1\.libs>dir
 Volume in drive G has no label.
 Volume Serial Number is FAEC-928D

 Directory of G:\Users\gmp-6.2.1\.libs

04/08/2023  01:10 AM    <DIR>          .
04/08/2023  01:10 AM    <DIR>          ..
04/08/2023  01:08 AM             1,384 assert.o
04/08/2023  01:08 AM             1,100 compat.o
04/08/2023  01:08 AM             1,240 errno.o
04/08/2023  01:08 AM             1,123 extract-dbl.o
04/08/2023  01:08 AM               912 invalid.o
04/08/2023  01:10 AM           671,944 libgmp-10.dll
04/08/2023  01:10 AM            16,660 libgmp-3.dll.def
04/08/2023  01:10 AM           385,280 libgmp.dll.a
04/08/2023  01:10 AM               878 libgmp.la
04/08/2023  01:10 AM               886 libgmp.lai
04/08/2023  01:10 AM             6,538 libgmpxx-3.dll.def
04/08/2023  01:10 AM            81,492 libgmpxx-4.dll
04/08/2023  01:10 AM            71,872 libgmpxx.dll.a
04/08/2023  01:10 AM               914 libgmpxx.la
04/08/2023  01:10 AM               918 libgmpxx.lai
04/08/2023  01:08 AM             1,929 memory.o
04/08/2023  01:08 AM               815 mp_bpl.o
04/08/2023  01:08 AM               450 mp_clz_tab.o
04/08/2023  01:08 AM             1,162 mp_dv_tab.o
04/08/2023  01:09 AM             1,681 mp_get_fns.o
04/08/2023  01:08 AM               813 mp_minv_tab.o
04/08/2023  01:09 AM             2,523 mp_set_fns.o
04/08/2023  01:09 AM             1,714 nextprime.o
04/08/2023  01:09 AM             3,160 primesieve.o
04/08/2023  01:09 AM             1,591 tal-reent.o
04/08/2023  01:09 AM               692 version.o
              26 File(s)      1,259,671 bytes
               2 Dir(s)   3,459,497,984 bytes free

G:\Users\gmp-6.2.1\.libs>
```

Now let's call the `lib` utility to generate `.lib` files:

```
G:\Users\gmp-6.2.1\.libs>lib /def:libgmp-3.dll.def
↪  /out:libgmp-3.lib
Microsoft (R) Library Manager Version 14.31.31107.0
Copyright (C) Microsoft Corporation.  All rights reserved.
```

```
LINK : warning LNK4068: /MACHINE not specified; defaulting to X64
   Creating library libgmp-3.lib and object libgmp-3.exp

G:\Users\gmp-6.2.1\.libs>lib /def:libgmpxx-3.dll.def
↪   /out:libgmpxx-3.lib
Microsoft (R) Library Manager Version 14.31.31107.0
Copyright (C) Microsoft Corporation.  All rights reserved.

LINK : warning LNK4068: /MACHINE not specified; defaulting to X64
   Creating library libgmpxx-3.lib and object libgmpxx-3.exp
```

Once again looking at the contents of the directory, make sure that the required files have appeared:

```
G:\Users\gmp-6.2.1\.libs>dir
 Volume in drive G has no label.
 Volume Serial Number is FAEC-928D

 Directory of G:\Users\gmp-6.2.1\.libs

04/08/2023  02:43 AM    <DIR>          .
04/08/2023  02:43 AM    <DIR>          ..
04/08/2023  01:08 AM             1,384 assert.o
04/08/2023  01:08 AM             1,100 compat.o
04/08/2023  01:08 AM             1,240 errno.o
04/08/2023  01:08 AM             1,123 extract-dbl.o
04/08/2023  01:08 AM               912 invalid.o
04/08/2023  01:10 AM           671,944 libgmp-10.dll
04/08/2023  01:10 AM            16,660 libgmp-3.dll.def
04/08/2023  02:41 AM            77,641 libgmp-3.exp
04/08/2023  02:41 AM           130,122 libgmp-3.lib
04/08/2023  01:10 AM           385,280 libgmp.dll.a
04/08/2023  01:10 AM               878 libgmp.la
04/08/2023  01:10 AM               886 libgmp.lai
04/08/2023  01:10 AM             6,538 libgmpxx-3.dll.def
04/08/2023  02:43 AM            23,097 libgmpxx-3.exp
04/08/2023  02:43 AM            29,040 libgmpxx-3.lib
04/08/2023  01:10 AM            81,492 libgmpxx-4.dll
04/08/2023  01:10 AM            71,872 libgmpxx.dll.a
04/08/2023  01:10 AM               914 libgmpxx.la
04/08/2023  01:10 AM               918 libgmpxx.lai
04/08/2023  01:08 AM             1,929 memory.o
04/08/2023  01:08 AM               815 mp_bpl.o
04/08/2023  01:08 AM               450 mp_clz_tab.o
04/08/2023  01:08 AM             1,162 mp_dv_tab.o
04/08/2023  01:09 AM             1,681 mp_get_fns.o
04/08/2023  01:08 AM               813 mp_minv_tab.o
04/08/2023  01:09 AM             2,523 mp_set_fns.o
04/08/2023  01:09 AM             1,714 nextprime.o
04/08/2023  01:09 AM             3,160 primesieve.o
04/08/2023  01:09 AM             1,591 tal-reent.o
04/08/2023  01:09 AM               692 version.o
              30 File(s)      1,519,571 bytes
```

2 Dir(s)   3,459,022,848 bytes free

G:\Users\gmp-6.2.1\.libs>

The files `libgmp-3.lib` and `libgmpxx-3.lib` should be copied to the directory `Programs\msys\local\lib`.

There is also the so-called `mini-gmp`, a compact implementation of the mpn and mpz GMP interfaces. It can be used when you need to work with numbers that do not fit into the machine word, but there is no need for highly efficient work with very large numbers. Applications can use `mini-gmp`, which has a GMP-compliant interface, with minimal effort. You can also link the application conditionally with GMP and use `mini-gmp` as a fallback option—for the case when, for some reason, GMP is not available or is undesirable as a dependency. The performance of `mini-gmp` is at least ten times slower than GMP when dealing with numbers represented by a few hundred bits. There are no asymptotically fast algorithms in `mini-gmp`, so when dealing with very large numbers, `mini-gmp` is many orders of magnitude slower than GMP.

The supported subset of GMP interfaces is declared in the `mini-gmp.h` header file. Function implementations are fully compatible with the corresponding GMP functions, with a few exceptions:

`mpz_set_str`, `mpz_init_set_str`, `mpz_get_str`, `mpz_out_str`, and `mpz_sizeinbase` only support $|base| <= 36$; `mpz_export` and `mpz_import` only support `NAILS=0`.

The `REALLOC_FUNC` and `FREE_FUNC` functions registered by the `mp_set_memory_functions` function do not receive the correct allocated memory block size in the corresponding argument. `mini-gmp` always sends null for these rarely used arguments.

The `mini-gmp` implementation consists of a single `mini-gmp.c` file and does not need to be installed. You can use the `#include mini-gmp.c` directive (some problems with macro and function definitions may occur), or you can include the `#include mini-gmp.h` header file and include `mini-gmp.c` in the list of separately compiled units.

12.1.1 GNU MPFR Library

The GNU MPFR Library (MPFR) is a library written in C for arbitrary-precision floating-point calculations with round-correct. MPFR is based on the GMP library and is maintained on a permanent basis by the INRIA resource (www.inria.fr); the current main developers are in the Caramel and AriC projects from the LORIA (Nancy, France) and LIP (Lyon, France) laboratories, respectively.

The main goal of this library is to provide an efficient library for high-precision floating-point calculations with a user-friendly interface. The library uses the useful ideas of the ANSI/IEEE-754 standard for double-precision floating-point arithmetic with 53 significant bits.

MPFR is a free library distributed under the GNU Lesser General Public License (GNU Lesser GPL, GNU LGPL, www.gnu.org/copyleft/lesser.html), version 3 or higher (2.1 or higher for MPFR versions prior to 2.4.x). This license guarantees the freedom to distribute and modify the MPFR library and is freely available to everyone. Unlike the General Public License, the LGPL allows commercial application developers to use the MPFR library.

The library is widely used by a number of free and commercial software, including GCC (GNU Compiler Collection), FLINT (Fast Library for Number Theory), Multiprecision Computing Toolbox for MATLAB, as well as one of the leading mathematical packages Waterloo Maple since version 11 (via the RS library).

There are a number of C++ interfaces for MPFR: MPFRCPP, MPFR C++ wrapper, `mpfr::real` class, and `gmpfrxx` C++ for both GMP and MPFR. The well-known Boost library includes an interface to MPFR as part of its arbitrary-precision library. Note also the RandomLib MPFR interface (C++ classes).

There are also interfaces for Eiffel, R, Perl (Math::MPFR), Python, and LISP languages. The functional programming language Ursala and the Racket language also have MPFR interfaces.

In addition, bindings are available from Python for GMP, MPFR, and MPC (`gmpy2`), Haskell for MPFR (`hmpfr`), Ruby for GMP and MPFR, Ada for GMP and MPFR, and Java for MPFR.

Links to these resources can be found on the library's website. Library documentation can be found at [32].

The official website is www.mpfr.org. The building of the library is carried out according to the standard scheme, like GMP.

12.2   Example: Computation of 10 000 000!

As an example of using the GMP library, let's take the simplest program for calculating 10000000! in a direct (non-recursive) way: sequentially multiplying by the next integer up to 10000000.

$$10000000! = 1 \cdot 2 \cdot 3 \cdots 10000000.$$

Note Once again, we strongly recommend that you rebuild the GMP library on the same machine that will be used for computing to achieve maximum computing performance.

By including the `<chrono>` header file, we enable time manipulation facilities. Of undoubted interest is the calculation time of 10000000! The following code fragment

```
steady_clock::time_point start = steady_clock::now();
for (int i=2; i<=N; ++i)
```

```
      fact *= i;
steady_clock::time_point end = steady_clock::now();
```

fixes the start and end points of the calculations. Further, their difference is given in a suitable format; in this case, the result is in seconds. To get the result in microseconds or nanoseconds, you can include the following lines in your code:

```
cout << duration_cast<microseconds>(end - start).count() <<
↪   "mcs\n";
```

and

```
cout << duration_cast<nanoseconds>(end - start).count() <<
↪   "ns\n";
```

Here is the complete program code:

```
/*
g++ '10000000!.cpp' -I/local/include -L/local/lib -o
↪   '10000000!.exe' -lgmp -lgmpxx -std=c++11
Put libgmp-10.dll and libgmpxx-4.dll in the folder where
↪   10000000!.exe is located
*/

#include <iostream>
#include <chrono>
#include <gmpxx.h>

using namespace std;
using namespace std::chrono;

const int N = 10000000;

int main(){

    mpz_class fact = 1;

    steady_clock::time_point start = steady_clock::now();
    for (int i=2; i<=N; ++i)
       fact *= i;
    steady_clock::time_point end = steady_clock::now();
    cout << "Calculated in: " << endl;
    cout << duration_cast<seconds>(end - start).count() << "s\n";

    cout << N << "! = " << fact.get_str(10) << "\n";
    return 0;
}
```

In our case, we compiled the code with the MinGW compiler version 4.8.1 (to emphasize the relevance of even not the latest versions of this compiler), so we used the -std=c++11 option. With more recent versions of this compiler, this option is generally not needed and can be omitted:

```
$ g++ '10000000!.cpp' -I/local/include -L/local/lib -o
↪  '10000000!.exe' -lgmp -lgmpxx -std=c++11
```

The program will require dynamic libraries `libgmp-10.dll` and `libgmpxx-4.dll` to run. Either add the directory where these files are located to your PATH variable or place these files next to your executable.

Since 10,000,000! is a very large number, we do not recommend running the program in the usual way, displaying the result directly on the screen. Instead, it's better to redirect the output to a file with the command

```
$ ./'10000000!.exe' > '10000000!.txt'
```

After some time, which depends on the power of your computer, a file 10000000!.txt with a size of about 64 MB will be created in the current directory. The first four lines of our file contain lines with calculation times in seconds, microseconds, and nanoseconds (we added output in microseconds and nanoseconds). To display only them, you need to give the command

```
$ head -4 '10000000!.txt'
Calculated in:
14990s
14990356164mcs
14990356164858ns
```

Such a long (almost 4 h) computation time is explained by the fact that we performed the calculations on an Asus N56VJ laptop (Intel64 Family 6 Model 58 Stepping 9 GenuineIntel 2401 Mhz, 16 GB RAM) with a 64-bit Windows 8 operating system. On more modern machines, computation time is significantly lower.

12.3   Conclusion

In this chapter, we showed how to build the very popular GNU Multiprecision Library (GMP) for working with very large numbers using MSYS and MinGW and gave recommendations on how to use it. Once again, we emphasized that we recommend building this library on the target machine whenever you are going to perform calculations on this particular machine. As an example of using this library, we have given the source code of a C++ program that calculates 10,000,000! (ten million factorial).

Crypto++

13

Crypto++ (also called CryptoPP, libcrypto++, and libcryptopp) is a cross-platform, free, and open source cryptographic C++ library written by Wei Dai.

The official website is www.cryptopp.com, and the latest version at the time of this writing is Crypto++ Library 8.7 (www.cryptopp.com/cryptopp870.zip).

The library is widely used in academic, student, commercial, noncommercial, and open source projects. First released in 1995, the library fully supports 32-bit and 64-bit architectures for most common operating systems and platforms, including Android, Apple (Mac OS X and iOS), BSD, Cygwin, IBM AIX, and S/390, Linux, MinGW, Solaris, Windows, Windows Phone and Windows RT.

Compilation according to C++03, C++11, and C++17 standards is supported; many compilers and IDEs, including Borland Turbo C++, Borland C++ Builder, Clang, CodeWarrior Pro, GCC (including Apple's GCC), Intel C++ Compiler (ICC), Microsoft C/C++ Compiler, and Sun Studio, are supported. In particular, the current version of Crypto++ supports the following compilers and IDEs:

Visual Studio 2003–2022
GCC 3.3–7.2
Apple Clang 4.3–8.3
LLVM Clang 2.9–4.0
C++Builder 2010
Intel C++ Compiler 9–16.0
Sun Studio 12u1–12.5
IBM XL C/C++ 10.0–13.1

B. I. Tuleuov, A. B. Ospanova, *Beginning C++ Compilers*, https://doi.org/10.1007/978-1-4842-9563-2_13

According to the documentation, the library covers the following algorithms:

Algorithm	Name
Authenticated encryption schemes	GCM, CCM, EAX
High-speed stream ciphers	ChaCha (8/12/20), Panama, Sosemanuk, Salsa20 (8/12/20), XSalsa20
AES and AES candidates	AES (Rijndael), RC6, MARS, Twofish, Serpent, CAST-256
Other block ciphers	ARIA, IDEA, Blowfish, Triple-DES (DES-EDE2 and DES-EDE3), Camellia, SEED, Kalyna (128/256/512), RC5, SIMON-64 and SIMON-128, SPECK-64 and SPECK-128, SM4, Threefish (256/512/1024), Skipjack, SHACAL-2, TEA, XTEA
Block cipher modes	ECB, CBC, CBC ciphertext stealing (CTS), CFB, OFB, counter mode (CTR)
Message authentication codes	BLAKE2b and BLAKE2s, CMAC, CBC-MAC, DMAC, GMAC (GCM), HMAC, Poly1305, SipHash, Two-Track-MAC, VMAC
Hash functions	BLAKE2b and BLAKE2s, Keccak (F1600), SHA-1, SHA-2, SHA-3, Poly1305, SipHash, Tiger, RIPEMD (128, 256, 160, 320), SM3, WHIRLPOOL
Public key cryptography	RSA, DSA, Deterministic DSA (RFC 6979), ElGamal, Nyberg-Rueppel (NR), Rabin-Williams (RW), EC-based German Digital Signature (ECGDSA), LUC, LUCELG, DLIES (DHAES variants), ESIGN
Padding schemes for public key systems	PKCS#1 v2.0, OAEP, PSS, PSSR, IEEE P1363 EMSA2 and EMSA5
Key agreement schemes	Diffie-Hellman (DH), Unified Diffie-Hellman (DH2), Menezes-Qu-Vanstone (MQV), Hashed MQV (HMQV), Fully Hashed MQV (FHMQV), LUCDIF, XTR- DH
Elliptic-curve cryptography	ECDSA, Deterministic ECDSA (RFC 6979), ECGDSA, ECNR, ECIES, ECDH, ECMQV
Insecure or obsolete algorithms left for backward compatibility and historical significance	MD2, MD4, MD5, Panama Hash, DES, ARC4, SEAL 3.0, WAKE-OFB, DESX (DES-XEX3), RC2, SAFER, 3-WAY , GOST, SHARK, CAST-128, Square

The library also includes

Pseudo random number generators (PRNGs): ANSI X9.17 Appendix C, RandomPool, VIA Padlock, RDRAND, RDSEED, NIST Hash, and HMAC DRBGs

Password-based key derivation functions: PBKDF1 and PBKDF2 from PKCS#5, PBKDF from PKCS#12 Appendix B, HKDF from RFC 5869

Shamir's Secret Information Sharing Scheme and Rabin's Information Dispersal Algorithm (IDA)

Fast arbitrary-precision integer arithmetic (bignum) and polynomial operations

Finite field arithmetic, including $GF(p)$ and $GF(2^n)$

Generating and testing prime numbers

Useful non-cryptographic algorithms

Compression/decompression of information according to the DEFLATE specification (RFC 1951) with support for gzip (RFC 1952) and zlib (RFC 1950) formats

Hexadecimal, base-32, base-64, and URL-safe base-64 encoding and decoding

Algorithm checksums 32-bit CRC, CRC-C, and Adler32

Wrapper classes for specific components of the following operating systems (optional):

High-resolution timers for Windows, Unix, and Mac OS

Berkeley and Windows sockets

Windows Named Pipes

/dev/random, /dev/urandom, /dev/srandom

Microsoft's CryptGenRandom and BCryptGenRandom for Windows

x86, x64 (x86-64), x32 (ILP32), ARM-32, Aarch32, Aarch64, and Power8 in-core code for the commonly used algorithms

Dynamic detection of processor properties and code selection

Support for GCC- and MSVC-style inline assembly, as well as MASM x64

x86, x64 (x86-64), and x32 platforms implement MMX, SSE2, and SSE4 technologies

ARM-32, Aarch32, and Aarch64 platforms implement NEON, ASIMD, and ARMv8 technologies

Power8 provides in-core AES using NX Crypto Acceleration

High-level interface to most of the above, using the filter/pipe metaphor

Performance tests and validations

13.1   Building with MinGW

The library is easily built following the instructions from the documentation:

In general, all you should have to do is open a terminal, cd to the cryptopp directory, and then:

```
make
make test
sudo make install
```

The command above builds the static library and cryptest.exe program. It also uses a sane default flags, which are usually "-DNDEBUG -g2 -O3 -fPIC". If you want to build the shared object, then issue:

```
make static dynamic cryptest.exe
```

Or:

```
make libcryptopp.a libcryptopp.so cryptest.exe
```

With the following three commands, we sequentially set the path to the executable files of the MinGW 8.1 compiler, MSYS, and launch the `bash` shell from MSYS, respectively:

```
G:\>mingw81
G:\>msys
G:\>bash
```

To build the library with the MinGW compiler, create the `G:\Users\MinGW\cryptopp870` folder and unpack the archive into this directory:

```
bash-3.1$ cd /G/Users/MinGW/cryptopp870

bash-3.1$ make static dynamic cryptest.exe

bash-3.1$ make test
. . .
passed      crypto_box_keypair pairwise consistency
passed      crypto_sign, crypto_sign_open, crypto_sign_keypair
passed      crypto_sign_keypair pairwise consistency

All tests passed!

Seed used was 1681125972
Test started at Mon Apr 10 14:26:12 2023
Test ended at Mon Apr 10 14:26:48 2023
bash-3.1$

bash-3.1$ make install
cp *.h /usr/local/include/cryptopp
chmod u=rw,go=r /usr/local/include/cryptopp/*.h
cp libcryptopp.a /usr/local/lib
chmod u=rw,go=r /usr/local/lib/libcryptopp.a
cp libcryptopp.so /usr/local/lib
chmod u=rwx,go=rx /usr/local/lib/libcryptopp.so
cp cryptest.exe /usr/local/bin
chmod u=rwx,go=rx /usr/local/bin/cryptest.exe
cp TestData/*.dat /usr/local/share/cryptopp/TestData
chmod u=rw,go=r /usr/local/share/cryptopp/TestData/*.dat
cp TestVectors/*.txt /usr/local/share/cryptopp/TestVectors
chmod u=rw,go=r /usr/local/share/cryptopp/TestVectors/*.txt
bash-3.1$
```

13.2   Building with Microsoft C/C++ Compiler

Now, to build the library with the Microsoft C/C++ compiler, create the `G:\Users\MSVC\cryptopp870` directory and extract the archive there:

```
C:\Users\User>X:
```

```
X:\>LaunchBuildEnv.cmd amd64
*****************************************************************
** Enterprise Windows Driver Kit (WDK) build environment
** Version ni_release_svc_prod1.22621.382
*****************************************************************
** Visual Studio 2022 Developer Command Prompt v17.1.5
** Copyright (c) 2022 Microsoft Corporation
*****************************************************************
X:\>

X:\>cd /d G:\Users\MSVC\cryptopp870

G:\Users\MSVC\cryptopp870>MSBuild cryptest.sln
↪  /p:Configuration=release /p:Platform=x64
. . .
Build succeeded.
    0 Warning(s)
    0 Error(s)

Time Elapsed 00:04:05.19

G:\Users\MSVC\cryptopp870>
```

13.3   Example: AES Implementation

Implementation of the AES symmetric encryption algorithm in CBC mode

```cpp
/*
Crypto++AES.cpp
*/

#include <iostream>
#include <iomanip>
#include "cryptopp/modes.h"
#include "cryptopp/aes.h"
#include "cryptopp/filters.h"

int main(int argc, char* argv[]){
    //Key and IV setup
    //AES encryption uses a secret key of a variable length
    ↪  (128-bit,
    //196-bit or 256-bit). This key is secretly exchanged between
    ↪  two
    //parties before communication begins. DEFAULT_KEYLENGTH= 16
    ↪  bytes
    CryptoPP::byte key[CryptoPP::AES::DEFAULT_KEYLENGTH],
      iv[CryptoPP::AES::BLOCKSIZE];
    memset(key, 0x00, CryptoPP::AES::DEFAULT_KEYLENGTH);
    memset(iv, 0x00, CryptoPP::AES::BLOCKSIZE);
    //
    // String and Sink setup
    //
```

```
std::string plaintext = "Now is the time for all good men to
↪  come to the aide...";
std::string ciphertext;
std::string decryptedtext;
//
// Dump Plain Text
//
std::cout << "Plain Text (" << plaintext.size() << " bytes)"
↪  << std::endl;
std::cout << plaintext;
std::cout << std::endl << std::endl;
//
// Create Cipher Text
//
CryptoPP::AES::Encryption aesEncryption(key,
  CryptoPP::AES::DEFAULT_KEYLENGTH);
CryptoPP::CBC_Mode_ExternalCipher::Encryption
  cbcEncryption(aesEncryption, iv);

CryptoPP::StreamTransformationFilter
↪  stfEncryptor(cbcEncryption,
  new CryptoPP::StringSink(ciphertext));
stfEncryptor.Put(reinterpret_cast<const unsigned
↪  char*>(plaintext.c_str()), plaintext.length() + 1);
stfEncryptor.MessageEnd();
//
// Dump Cipher Text
//
std::cout << "Cipher Text (" << ciphertext.size() << "
↪  bytes)" << std::endl;

for (int i = 0; i < ciphertext.size(); i++){
    std::cout << "0x" << std::hex << (0xFF &
    ↪  static_cast<CryptoPP::byte>(ciphertext[i])) << " ";
}

std::cout << std::endl << std::endl;
//
// Decrypt
//
CryptoPP::AES::Decryption aesDecryption(key,
  CryptoPP::AES::DEFAULT_KEYLENGTH);
CryptoPP::CBC_Mode_ExternalCipher::Decryption
  cbcDecryption(aesDecryption, iv);

CryptoPP::StreamTransformationFilter
↪  stfDecryptor(cbcDecryption,
  new CryptoPP::StringSink(decryptedtext));
stfDecryptor.Put(reinterpret_cast<const unsigned
↪  char*>(ciphertext.c_str()), ciphertext.size());
stfDecryptor.MessageEnd();
//
// Dump Decrypted Text
```

```
//
std::cout << "Decrypted Text: " << std::endl;
std::cout << decryptedtext;
std::cout << std::endl << std::endl;

return 0;
}
```

We now give commands for building this program for a different set of tools.

Using the MinGW compiler and MSYS package We remind you that when building with MSYS using the `make install` command from under bash, the header files and the finished built library are copied (installed) to the `local/include` and `local/lib` subdirectories of the MSYS tree, respectively:

```
G:\>mingw81
G:\>msys
G:\>bash
bash-3.1$ g++ Crypto++AES.cpp -I/local/include -L/local/lib
↪  -lcryptopp -o Crypto++AES.exe
```

With the MinGW compiler and without the MSYS package If MSYS is installed in, say, `E:\Programs\MSYS`, and we are not running a `bash` shell emulator, then the aforementioned header files and compiled library directories must already be set in Windows format:

```
G:\>mingw81
> g++ Crypto++AES.cpp -I"E:\Programs\MSYS\local\include"
↪  -L"E:\Programs\MSYS\local\lib" -lcryptopp -o Crypto++AES.exe
```

Using the Microsoft C/C++ compiler, assuming that the header files are in the `E:\Programs\Include` directory and the compiled `cryptlib.lib` library is in the same directory as the `Crypto++AES.cpp` source code file:

```
>LaunchBuildEnv.cmd
>vc.bat 64
> set INCLUDE=E:\Programs\Include;%INCLUDE%
> cl Crypto++AES.cpp cryptlib.lib
```

Now let's run the compiled program:

```
bash-3.1$ Crypto++AES.exe
Plain Text (55 bytes)
Now is the time for all good men to come to the aide...

Cipher Text (64 bytes)
```

```
0x7f 0xf8 0xb3 0xea 0x8a 0x2 0xb3 0x7a 0x3d 0x28 0x66
  ↪   0x9c 0x97 0x13 0xa7 0xb3 0xf 0xa2 0x50 0x25 0x80
  ↪   0xd5 0xd2 0x32 0xce 0xe8 0xa 0x57 0x33 0xef 0x70
  ↪   0xff 0x48 0xe9 0xe8 0x4 0x98 0xa9 0x4 0xc2 0x5e
  ↪   0xa7 0xb0 0x40 0x43 0xa1 0xfc 0x23 0xb1 0xa1 0xeb
  ↪   0x1e 0xb2 0xf6 0x97 0x62 0x70 0xa1 0x81 0xca 0x6e
  ↪   0x78 0x80 0x90

Decrypted Text:
Now is the time for all good men to come to the aide...

bash-3.1$
```

13.4   Conclusion

In this chapter, we have shown how to compile the well-known cryptographic library Crypto++ using the MinGW and Microsoft C/C++ compilers.

As a demonstration of the use of the library, an example of a program that implements the AES encryption algorithm was given.

OpenSSL

14

OpenSSL is a popular open source cross-platform cryptographic library. In addition to well-known cryptographic algorithms and hash functions, the library also implements the SSL and TLS protocols; many sites on the Internet that use the HTTPS protocol use this library.

The library can be downloaded from the official website (www.openssl.org) in source code. Version 3.1.0 can be downloaded through www.openssl.org/source/openssl-3.1.0.tar.gz.

OpenSSL can be built under Windows with both the Microsoft C/C++ and MinGW compilers, and the build process is not very time consuming, contrary to popular belief.

14.1   Building with MinGW

Building the library with the MinGW compiler naturally requires MSYS. The first version of MSYS, unfortunately, is not suitable due to the version of the Perl interpreter included in it:

```
bash-3.1$ ./Configure mingw64
Perl v5.10.0 required--this is only v5.8.8, stopped at
↪   ./Configure line 12.
BEGIN failed--compilation aborted at ./Configure line 12.
```

The situation is not saved by another free implementation of the Perl interpreter—Strawberry Perl:

```
*****************************************************************
This perl implementation doesn't produce Unix like paths
(with forward slash directory separators). Please use an
implementation that matches your building platform.

This Perl version: 5.32.1 for MSWin32-x64-multi-thread
*****************************************************************
```

© The Author(s), under exclusive license to APress Media, LLC,
part of Springer Nature 2024
B. I. Tuleuov, A. B. Ospanova, *Beginning C++ Compilers*,
https://doi.org/10.1007/978-1-4842-9563-2_14

This is where MSYS2 comes to the rescue. We remind you that this environment has its own package manager, which allows you to install the missing packages (programs) on the fly. In the MSYS2 environment, building the library is extremely simple; we will describe this process step by step. Copy the downloaded archive of the `openssl-3.1.0.tar.gz` library, for example, to the `E:\Users` directory and start the MSYS2 environment with our `msys2[.bat]` command and go to this directory in the MSYS2 environment (pay attention to the path entry format):

```
Berik@Berik-Mobile MSYS ~
$ cd /e/Users

Berik@Berik-Mobile MSYS /e/Users
$ls
openssl-3.1.0.tar.gz
```

Now unpack the archive and go to the directory with the source code of the library:

```
Berik@Berik-Mobile MSYS /e/Users
$ tar zxf openssl-3.1.0.tar.gz && cd openssl-3.1.0
```

Let's select the version of the MinGW compiler. Note: `'f'` stands for the drive letter where our `Programs` directory is located; you must replace it with the drive letter of your `Programs` directory!

```
Berik@Berik-Mobile MSYS /e/Users/openssl-3.1.0
$ export PATH=/f/Programs/mingw64-8.1.0/bin:$PATH
```

In the files `INSTALL.md`, `NOTES-UNIX.md`, `NOTES-WINDOWS.md`, and `README.md`, you can find information on building and using the library; for further work, we will run the `Configure` script:

```
Berik@Berik-Mobile MSYS /e/Users/openssl-3.1.0
$ ./Configure mingw64
Configuring OpenSSL version 3.1.0 for target mingw64
Using os-specific seed configuration
Created configdata.pm
Running configdata.pm
Created Makefile.in
Created Makefile
Created include/openssl/configuration.h


**********************************************************************
**                                                                ***
**    OpenSSL has been successfully configured                    ***
**                                                                ***
**    If you encounter a problem while building, please open an   ***
**    issue on GitHub <https://github.com/openssl/openssl/issues> ***
**    and include the output from the following command:          ***
**                                                                ***
**        perl configdata.pm --dump                               ***
**                                                                ***
**    (If you are new to OpenSSL, you might want to consult the   ***
**    'Troubleshooting' section in the INSTALL.md file first)     ***
```

**   ***
****

Further commands are completely straightforward, these are building, testing and installation of the library with sequential commands:

```
Berik@Berik-Mobile MSYS /e/Users/openssl-3.1.0
$ make

Berik@Berik-Mobile MSYS /e/Users/openssl-3.1.0
$ make test

Berik@Berik-Mobile MSYS /e/Users/openssl-3.1.0
$ make install
```

The library can be built by different versions of the MinGW compiler: for example, we also used MinGW version 4.8.1. Whenever building a library with a different compiler version, remember that the previous version will be overwritten by the new version.

14.2   Building with Microsoft C/C++ Compiler

To build the library, we need the Netwide Assembler and some implementations of the Perl interpreter, preferably free, and we suggest Strawberry Perl as such. Note that both of these packages work on older versions of Windows as well (we tested on Windows 7 SP1).

According to the official website (www.nasm.us) of the product:

Netwide Assembler (NASM), an assembler for the x86 CPU architecture portable to nearly every modern platform, and with code generation for many platforms old and new

We can choose to download from www.nasm.us/pub/nasm/releasebuilds/2.16.01/ win64:

```
nasm-2.16.01-installer-x64.exe  2022-12-21  1.0M  Installable
↪  package
nasm-2.16.01-win64.zip          2022-12-21  494K  Executable only
```

We, according to our settings, will choose the portable version: www.nasm.us/ pub/nasm/releasebuilds/2.16.01/win64/nasm-2.16.01-win64.zip.

Unpack this archive into the `Programs\nasm-2.16.01` directory and create a batch file `nasm.bat` to quickly launch the NASM environment, and, as always, place this file in the `Programs\bin` directory:

```
@echo off

set PATH=%~d0\Programs\nasm-2.16.01;%PATH%
```

Strawberry Perl, a free implementation of the Perl interpreter, is advertised by the creators on the product's official website (https://strawberryperl.com) as

> Strawberry Perl is a perl environment for MS Windows containing all you need to run and develop perl applications. It is designed to be as close as possible to perl environment on UNIX systems

Strawberry Perl comes in different flavors, which can be found at https://strawberryperl.com/releases.html. Again, we offer a portable version: https://strawberryperl.com/download/5.32.1.1/strawberry-perl-5.32.1.1-64bit-portable.zip.

Unpack this archive into the `Programs\Strawberry-Perl-5.32.1.1` directory, and in the `Programs\bin` directory, create a batch file `sperl.bat` to quickly launch the Perl environment:

```
@echo off
set "PerlDir=Programs\Strawberry-Perl-5.32.1.1"

set PATH=%~d0\%PerlDir%\perl\bin;%~d0\%PerlDir%\c\bin;%PATH%
set PATH=%~d0\%PerlDir%\perl\site\bin;%PATH%
```

We will place the downloaded `openssl-3.1.0.tar.gz` library archive, for example, in the `E:\Users` directory and run the `msys[.bat]` command and go to this directory:

```
C:\Users>msys

C:\Users>cd /d E:\Users
```

Now unpack the archive and go to the directory with the source code of the library:

```
E:\Users>tar zxf openssl-3.1.0.tar.gz && cd openssl-3.1.0

E:\Users\openssl-3.1.0>
```

Note We only need MSYS to unpack the `.tar.gz` archive. You can also use Far for this.

Now we sequentially run the batch files `nasm[.bat]` and `sperl[.bat]` to activate the Netwide Assembler environment and Strawberry Perl

```
E:\Users\openssl-3.1.0>nasm
E:\Users\openssl-3.1.0>sperl
```

Finally, we activate the EWDK environment with the command

```
E:\Users\openssl-3.1.0>vc 64
```

Here, we make an important remark. Our batch file `vc.bat` initializes the command line for compiling and building standard C/C++ programs. The OpenSSL library, when built under Windows, uses the Windows API and Windows Sockets functions, so we need to run the command

```
set INCLUDE=X:\Program Files\Windows
↪   Kits\10\Include\10.0.22621.0\um;X:\Program Files\Windows
↪   Kits\10\Include\10.0.22621.0\shared;%INCLUDE%
```

to avoid error messages about `winsock2.h` and `winapifamily.h` not being found. You also need to run the command

```
set PATH=X:\Program Files\Windows
↪   Kits\10\bin\10.0.22621.0\x64;%PATH%
```

to avoid the message that the resource compiler `rc.exe` was not found. Note that the drive letter `'X:'` means the drive letter where the ISO file or EWDK folder is mounted.

After all this, you can run the configure script:

```
E:\Users\openssl-3.1.0>perl Configure VC-WIN64A
```

which will generate a makefile to build the library and install it in the default directories. These directories are described in the documentation; here is a fragment of the `INSTALL.md` file:

```
### openssldir

    --openssldir=DIR

Directory for OpenSSL configuration files, and also the default
certificate and key store.  Defaults are:

    Unix:              /usr/local/ssl
    Windows:           C:\Program Files\Common Files\SSL
    OpenVMS:           SYS$COMMON:[OPENSSL-COMMON]

For 32bit Windows applications on Windows 64bit (WOW64), always
replace `C:\Program Files` by `C:\Program Files (x86)`.

### prefix

    --prefix=DIR

The top of the installation directory tree.  Defaults are:

    Unix:              /usr/local
    Windows:           C:\Program Files\OpenSSL
```

The directories are nested by default in the `C:\Program Files` directory, which is write-protected and requires you to run a command prompt with administrative privileges. For this reason, we will choose a different directory for installing the library: for the library itself, the `Programs\OpenSSL` folder and

`Programs\OpenSSL\SSL` for the configuration files. Therefore, we will call the Configure script with the following parameters:

```
E:\Users\openssl-3.1.0>perl Configure --prefix=G:\Programs\OpenSSL
↪   --openssldir=G:\Programs\OpenSSL\SSL VC-WIN64A
Configuring OpenSSL version 3.1.0 for target VC-WIN64A
Using os-specific seed configuration
Created configdata.pm
Running configdata.pm
Created makefile.in
Created makefile
Created include\openssl\configuration.h

**********************************************************************
*                                                                 ***
*    OpenSSL has been successfully configured                     ***
*                                                                 ***
*    If you encounter a problem while building, please open an    ***
*    issue on GitHub <https://github.com/openssl/openssl/issues>  ***
*    and include the output from the following command:           ***
*                                                                 ***
*        perl configdata.pm --dump                                ***
*                                                                 ***
*    (If you are new to OpenSSL, you might want to consult the    ***
*    'Troubleshooting' section in the INSTALL.md file first)      ***
*                                                                 ***
**********************************************************************
E:\Users\openssl-3.1.0>
```

Now just start building the library:

```
E:\Users\openssl-3.1.0>nmake
```

After the build is completed, we start testing the library:

```
E:\Users\openssl-3.1.0>nmake test
. . .
All tests successful.
Files=250, Tests=3168, 1521 wallclock secs (14.56 usr + 2.28 sys
↪   = 16.84 CPU)
Result: PASS
```

Finally, install the library with the command

```
E:\Users\openssl-3.1.0>nmake install
```

The library has now been successfully built and is ready to be used.

Possible pitfalls We note here a couple of non-obvious errors associated with the Microsoft C/C ++ compiler.

- If somehow the TMP environment variable is not set on your system, then the following error is possible:

```
cl : Command line error D8050 : cannot execute 'X:\Program
 ↪  Files\Microsoft Visual Studio\2019\BuildTools\VC\Tools\MS」
 ↪  VC\14.31.31103\bin\HostX64\x64\c1.dll': failed to get
 ↪  command line into debug records
NMAKE : fatal error U1077: '"X:\Program Files\Microsoft
 ↪  Visual Studio\2019\BuildTools\VC\Tools\MSVC\14.31.31103\b」
 ↪  in\HostX64\x64\cl.EXE"' : return code
 ↪  '0x2'
Stop.
NMAKE : fatal error U1077: '"X:\Program Files\Microsoft
 ↪  Visual Studio\2019\BuildTools\VC\Tools\MSVC\14.31.31103\b」
 ↪  in\HostX64\x64\nmake.exe"' : return code
 ↪  '0x2'
Stop.
```

- Run the command

```
E:\Users\openssl-3.1.0>vc 64
```

prior to the

```
E:\Users\openssl-3.1.0>perl Configure . . .
```

command; otherwise, it is possible to get the following error message, for example, under Windows 7 SP1:

> The program can't start because `mspdb100.dll` is missing from your computer. Try reinstalling the program to fix this problem

14.3 Conclusion

This chapter was about building with the MinGW and Microsoft C/C++ compilers another popular OpenSSL cryptographic library. Building with the Microsoft C/C++ compiler has some pitfalls; building with MinGW is extremely easy; however, this is the only case where we used MSYS2 and not MSYS.

Process Hacker

15

Process Hacker is a free and open source multipurpose utility created by enthusiasts. It is very useful for specialists in the field of system programming and computer and network security, developers when debugging software up to drivers, and just users, not necessarily even advanced ones.

For example, sometimes you need to find out which open file or resource does not allow you to delete a folder or close a window—Process Hacker will help you quickly find out.

The utility is designed to work in Windows 7 and higher; 32-bit and 64-bit versions are supported. The official website is https://processhacker.sourceforge.io.

Here are the key features of the utility, taken from the old official site:

- A detailed overview of system activity with highlighting.
- Graphs and statistics allow you to quickly track down resource hogs and runaway processes.
- Can't edit or delete a file? Discover which processes are using that file.
- See what programs have active network connections, and close them if necessary.
- Get real-time information on disk access.
- View detailed stack traces with kernel-mode, WOW64 and .NET support.
- Go beyond services.msc: create, edit, and control services.
- Small, portable, and no installation required.
- 100% free software (GPL v3).

Of course, such impressive functionality cannot be provided without the use of a kernel-mode driver, and Process Hacker includes a similar driver, KProcessHacker, whose source code is also freely available. As part of the source code of the utility,

B. I. Tuleuov, A. B. Ospanova, *Beginning C++ Compilers*, https://doi.org/10.1007/978-1-4842-9563-2_15

this driver is supplied already built with a certificate, due to the fact that, at the request of Microsoft, kernel-mode drivers must have a digitally signed certificate.[1]

The kernel-mode driver, according to the documentation, provides additional functionality, including

- Capturing kernel-mode stack traces
- More efficiently enumerating process handles
- Retrieving names for file handles
- Retrieving names for EtwRegistration objects
- Setting handle attributes

Since June 2022, the Process Hacker utility has been developed by Winsiderss and renamed to System Informer; Microsoft employees have appeared among the utility developers. One of the Process Hacker developers posted the following post (https://github.com/winsiderss/systeminformer/issues/1286):

The project is under maintenance while we migrate from Process Hacker to System Informer.
We ask the community to have patience while we migrate.

- Process Hacker is being renamed to System Informer. The project is now under Winsiderss. We are grateful for @ionescu007's and @yardenshafir's support.
- During this time, the master will be unstable. Please think carefully before opening new issues. Please try not to open issues related to the migration. The team may be slow to respond. We are not ignoring you.
- During this time, we ask that any feature requests, enhancements, or pull requests be held until after the migration. If you do create a feature request, we are likely "close as not planned," and we ask you to reopen it after the migration.

We are just as excited as you are to get an official 3.x release out.
There have been a number of opened issues for feature requests and/or bugs that are directly related to the instability of master due to migration effort or general issues opened asking, "What's going on?" We want to keep the discussion here open, but we will lock the project during the migration if it's necessary for us to focus.
We are doing our best to complete this by the end of the month.
Again, thank you for your patience. We'll be sure to provide updates as we can.

However, the source code for Process Hacker is available here: https://sourceforge.net/projects/processhacker. All versions, including the latest, can also be downloaded from https://sourceforge.net/projects/processhacker/files/processhacker2. As for System Informer, we believe that its functionality will be greatly reduced, and the functionality of Process Hacker is very rich; in addition, the utility has a rich set of plug-ins that can also be downloaded and built from source code.

---

[1] Of course, you can build this driver yourself, but you can use it without a signature, only putting Windows into test mode.

15.1 Building with Microsoft C/C++ Compiler

To build Process Hacker, you need Visual Studio version 2019 or later. For this, you need to run the `build_release.cmd` batch file from the build folder in the project root or open the `ProcessHacker.sln` files for the utility itself and `Plugins.sln` for plug-ins from the Visual Studio environment.

15.1.1 Building Driver

As we already mentioned, this step can be skipped. If necessary, the building of the driver is approximately the same as the utility itself.

15.1.2 Building Utility

We will build using MSBuild and EWDK. First, unzip the sources to a folder, say `J:\Users\processhacker-2.39-src`. At the root of this folder, there is a solution file `ProcessHacker.sln`, which we will process using the MSBuild. Mount EWDK on disk X: (see pages 96, 99, and 101) and activate the build environment:

```
X:\LaunchBuildEnv.cmd amd64
```

and change directory to

```
cd /d J:\Users\processhacker-2.39-src
```

If we immediately give the build command in this form

```
MSBuild ProcessHacker.sln /p:Configuration=Release
↪ /p:Platform=x64
```

then we get an error, because the default solution is configured to build with Visual Studio 2019 (`Platform Toolset = v142`), and in the EWDK we use, the value of this property is `143` (see Table 9-5). We will not fix the solution file, but set the property value on the command line:

```
MSBuild ProcessHacker.sln /p:Configuration=Release
↪ /p:Platform=x64 /p:PlatformToolset=v143
```

Next, the compiler will complain about missing files `windows.h`, `winapifamily.h`, and `ctype.h`. These files are located in directories (they can be easily found using Far Manager by going to drive X: and pressing `Alt` + `F7` keys):

```
X:\Program Files\Windows
↪ Kits\10\Include\10.0.22621.0\um\windows.h
X:\Program Files\Windows
↪ Kits\10\Include\10.0.22621.0\shared\winapifamily.h
```

and `ctype.h` can be found in two places at once:

```
X:\Program Files\Windows Kits\10\Include\10.0.22621.0\km\crt
X:\Program Files\Windows Kits\10\Include\10.0.22621.0\ucrt
```

These paths can again be passed through the command line by setting the property

```
/p:IncludePath="X:\Program Files\Windows
↪   Kits\10\Include\10.0.22621.0\um"
```

However, adding long paths to the command line is quite tedious, and you have to do it every time you build. Here, we will use the *responce* files (see page 105) and make this file called `ph.rsp`:

```
# ph.rsp responce file
# Not final version

/p:IncludePath="X:\Program Files\Windows
↪   Kits\10\Include\10.0.22621.0\um;X:\Program Files\Windows
↪   Kits\10\Include\10.0.22621.0\ucrt;X:\Program Files\ Windows
↪   Kits\10\Include\10.0.22621.0\shared;$(IncludePath)"
```

This file can be placed in the root folder next to the solution file.

Now we are ready to use this file:

```
MSBuild ProcessHacker.sln /p:Configuration=Release
↪   /p:Platform=x64 /p:PlatformToolset=v143 @ph.rsp
```

In the next step, we you will get compiler errors like

```
J:\Users\processhacker-2.39-src\phnt\include\ntpsapi.h(58,1):
↪   error C2220: the following warning is treated as an error
J:\Users\processhacker-2.39-src\phnt\include\ntpsapi.h(58,1):
↪   warning C4005: 'FLS_MAXIMUM_AVAILABLE': macro redefinition
```

The reason is the `FLS_MAXIMUM_AVAILABLE` macro is defined in both `winnt.h` (EWDK) and `ntpsapi.h` (Process Hacker). Generally, it is not an error, and it can be suppressed by setting compiler option (see page 186) `TreatWarningAsError` to False. However, MSBuild does not allow this option in the command line: neither `/p:TreatWarningAsError=False` nor `/p:DisableSpecificWarnings=C4005` property does not work!

However, there is a simple workaround here—setting the CL environment variable from the command line comes to the rescue here (see page 103)! Just run the command

```
set CL=/WX-
```

Note Next time, perform this prior to the `LaunchBuildEnv.cmd amd64` command.

After rerunning the command to build the solution, we now get linker errors for the absence of object library files `ntdll.lib`, `LIBCMT.lib`, and `libucrt.lib`. These files are located in the following folders:

```
X:\Program Files\Windows Kits\10\Lib\10.0.22621.0\um\x64
X:\Program Files\Microsoft Visual
↪  Studio\2022\BuildTools\VC\Tools\MSVC\14.31.31103\lib\x64
X:\Program Files\Windows Kits\10\Lib\10.0.22621.0\ucrt\x64
```

Again, these paths could be passed through the command line by defining the property

```
/p:LibraryPath="X:\Program Files\Windows
↪  Kits\10\Lib\10.0.22621.0\um\x64"
```

but we will do as we did with `IncludePath` by simply adding them to the `ph.rsp` responce file:

```
# ph.rsp responce file
# Final version

/p:IncludePath="X:\Program Files\Windows
↪  Kits\10\Include\10.0.22621.0\um;X:\Program Files\Windows
↪  Kits\10\Include\10.0.22621.0\ucrt;X:\Program Files\ Windows
↪  Kits\10\Include\10.0.22621.0\shared;$(IncludePath)"
/p:LibraryPath="X:\Program Files\Windows
↪  Kits\10\Lib\10.0.22621.0\um\x64;X:\Program Files\Microsoft
↪  Visual Studio\2022\BuildTools\VC\Tools\MSVC\14.31.31103
↪  \lib\x64;X:\Program Files\Windows
↪  Kits\10\Lib\10.0.22621.0\ucrt\x64;$(LibraryPath)"
```

Further, the Process Hacker build process does not cause problems.

Note If your EWDK is mounted on a different drive, change the drive letter `X:` in the `ph.rsp` responce file to yours.

15.2 Conclusion

In this chapter, we have shown in detail how to build the well-known Process Hacker utility with a kernel-mode driver using the EWDK. The source code of the utility is a set of Visual Studio projects combined into a solution; to build, we used the MSBuild build system. We have shown how to avoid possible errors that may occur when using the default EWDK environment settings.

Appendix

A

Visual Studio Version and Discrimination Macros

The material in this section is based on data from the site [29].

CL Task

This wraps the Microsoft C++ compiler tool, *cl.exe*. The compiler produces executable (*.exe*) files, dynamic-link library (*.dll*) files, or code module (*.netmodule*) files. For more information, see Compiler options and Use MSBuild from the command line and Use the Microsoft C++ toolset from the command line.

Parameters

The following list describes the parameters of the **CL** task. Most task parameters, and a few sets of parameters, correspond to a command-line option:

- **AdditionalIncludeDirectories**
  Optional String[] parameter.
  Adds a directory to the list of directories that are searched for include files.
  For more information, see /I (additional include directories).

© The Author(s), under exclusive license to APress Media, LLC, part of Springer Nature 2024
B. I. Tuleuov, A. B. Ospanova, *Beginning C++ Compilers*,
https://doi.org/10.1007/978-1-4842-9563-2

Table A-1 Visual Studio and Microsoft C/C++ compiler versions

Abbreviation	Product	VC++ Version	_MSC_VER	_MSC_FULL_VER
2022	Visual Studio 2022 version 17.3.4	14.30	1933	193331630
2022	Visual Studio 2022 version 17.2.2	14.30	1932	193231329
2022	EWDK with Visual Studio Build Tools 17.1.5	14.30	1931	193131107
2022	Visual Studio 2022 version 17.0.2	14.30	1930	193030706
2022	Visual Studio 2022 version 17.0.1	14.30	1930	193030705
2019 Update 11	Visual Studio 2019 version 16.11.2	14.28	1929	192930133
2019	EWDK with Visual Studio Build Tools 16.9.2	14.28	1928	192829913
2019 Update 9	Visual Studio 2019 version 16.9.2	14.28	1928	192829913
2019 Update 8	Visual Studio 2019 version 16.8.2	14.28	1928	192829334
2019 Update 8	Visual Studio 2019 version 16.8.1	14.28	1928	192829333
2019 Update 7	Visual Studio 2019 version 16.7	14.27	1927	192729112
2019 Update 6	Visual Studio 2019 version 16.6.2	14.26	1926	192628806
2019 Update 5	Visual Studio 2019 version 16.5.1	14.25	1925	192528611
2019 Update 4	Visual Studio 2019 version 16.4.0	14.24	1924	192428314
2019 Update 3	Visual Studio 2019 version 16.3.2	14.21	1923	192328105
2019	EWDK for Windows 10, version 2004 with Visual Studio Build Tools 16.3	14.21	1923	1923281054
2019 Update 2	Visual Studio 2019 version 16.2.3	14.21	1922	192227905
2019 Update 1	Visual Studio 2019 version 16.1.2	14.21	1921	192127702
2019	Visual Studio 2019 version 16.0.0	14.20	1920	192027508
2017 Update 9	Visual Studio 2017 version 15.9.11	14.16	1916	191627030

(continued)

Table A-1 (continued)

Abbreviation	Product	VC++ Version	_MSC_VER	_MSC_FULL_VER
2017 Update 9	Visual Studio 2017 version 15.9.7	14.16	1916	191627027
2017 Update 9	Visual Studio 2017 version 15.9.5	14.16	1916	191627026
2017 Update 9	Visual Studio 2017 version 15.9.4	14.16	1916	191627025
2017 Update 9	Visual Studio 2017 version 15.9.1	14.16	1916	191627023
2017 Update 9	Visual Studio 2017 version 15.9.0	14.16	1916	
2017 Update 8	Visual Studio 2017 version 15.8.0	14.15	1915	
2017 Update 7	Visual Studio 2017 version 15.7.5	14.14	1914	191426433
2017 Update 7	Visual Studio 2017 version 15.7.3	14.14	1914	191426430
2017 Update 7	Visual Studio 2017 version 15.7.2	14.14	1914	191426429
2017 Update 7	Visual Studio 2017 version 15.7.1	14.14	1914	191426428
2017 Update 6	Visual Studio 2017 version 15.6.7	14.13	1913	191326132
2017 Update 6	Visual Studio 2017 version 15.6.6	14.13	1913	191326131
2017 Update 6	Visual Studio 2017 version 15.6.4	14.13	1913	191326129
2017 Update 6	Visual Studio 2017 version 15.6.3	14.13	1913	191326129
2017 Update 6	Visual Studio 2017 version 15.6.2	14.13	1913	191326128
2017 Update 6	Visual Studio 2017 version 15.6.1	14.13	1913	191326128
2017 Update 6	Visual Studio 2017 version 15.6.0	14.13	1913	191326128
2017 Update 5	Visual Studio 2017 version 15.5.7	14.12	1912	191225835
2017 Update 5	Visual Studio 2017 version 15.5.6	14.12	1912	191225835
2017 Update 5	Visual Studio 2017 version 15.5.4	14.12	1912	191225834
2017 Update 5	Visual Studio 2017 version 15.5.3	14.12	1912	191225834

(continued)

Table A-1 (continued)

Abbreviation	Product	VC++ Version	_MSC_VER	_MSC_FULL_VER
2017 Update 5	Visual Studio 2017 version 15.5.2	14.12	1912	191225831
2017 Update 4	Visual Studio 2017 version 15.4.5	14.11	1911	191125547
2017 Update 4	Visual Studio 2017 version 15.4.4	14.11	1911	191125542
2017 Update 3	Visual Studio 2017 version 15.3.3	14.11	1911	191125507
2017 Update 2[a]	Visual Studio 2017 version 15.2	14.10	1910	191025017
2017 Update 1[b]	Visual Studio 2017 version 15.1	14.10	1910	191025017
2017	Visual Studio 2017 version 15.0	14.10[c]	1910	191025017
2015 Update 3	Visual Studio 2015 Update 3 [14.0]	14.0	1900	190024210
2015 Update 2	Visual Studio 2015 Update 2 [14.0]	14.0	1900	190023918
2015 Update 1	Visual Studio 2015 Update 1 [14.0]	14.0	1900	190023506
2015	Visual Studio 2015 [14.0]	14.0	1900	190023026
2013 November CTP	Visual Studio 2013 November CTP [12.0]	12.0	1800	180021114
2013 Update 5	Visual Studio 2013 Update 5 [12.0]	12.0	1800	180040629
2013 Update 4	Visual Studio 2013 Update 4 [12.0]	12.0	1800	180031101
2013 Update 3	Visual Studio 2013 Update 3 [12.0]	12.0	1800	180030723
2013 Update 2	Visual Studio 2013 Update 2 [12.0]	12.0	1800	180030501
2013 Update2 RC	Visual Studio 2013 Update2 RC [12.0]	12.0	1800	180030324
2013 Update 1[d]	Visual Studio 2013 Update 1 [12.0]	12.0	1800	180021005
2013	Visual Studio 2013 [12.0]	12.0	1800	180021005
2013 RC	Visual Studio 2013 RC [12.0]	12.0	1800	180020827
2013 Preview	Visual Studio 2013 Preview [12.0]	12.0	1800	180020617
2012 November CTP	Visual Studio 2012 November CTP [11.0]	11.0	1700	170051025

(continued)

Table A-1   (continued)

Abbreviation	Product	VC++ Version	_MSC_VER	_MSC_FULL_VER
2012 Update 4	Visual Studio 2012 Update 4 [11.0]	11.0	1700	170061030
2012 Update 3	Visual Studio 2012 Update 3 [11.0]	11.0	1700	170060610
2012 Update 2	Visual Studio 2012 Update 2 [11.0]	11.0	1700	170060315
2012 Update 1	Visual Studio 2012 Update 1 [11.0]	11.0	1700	170051106
2012	Visual Studio 2012 [11.0]	11.0	1700	170050727
2010 SP1	Visual Studio 2010 SP1 [10.0] Visual C++ 2010 SP1 [10.0]	10.0	1600	160040219
2010	Visual Studio 2010 [10.0] Visual C++ 2010 [10.0]	10.0	1600	160030319
2010 Beta 2	Visual Studio 2010 Beta 2 [10.0]	10.0	1600	160021003
2010 Beta 1	Visual Studio 2010 Beta 1 [10.0]	10.0	1600	160020506
2008 SP1	Visual Studio 2008 SP1 [9.0] Visual C++ 2008 SP1 [9.0]	9.0	1500	150030729
2008	Visual Studio 2008 [9.0] Visual C++ 2008 [9.0]	9.0	1500	150021022
2008 Beta 2	Visual Studio 2008 Beta 2 [9.0]	9.0	1500	150020706
2005 SP1	Visual Studio 2005 SP1 [8.0] Visual C++ 2005 SP1 [8.0]	8.0	1400	140050727
2005	Visual Studio 2005 [8.0] Visual C++ 2005 [8.0]	8.0	1400	140050320
2005 Beta 2	Visual Studio 2005 Beta 2 [8.0]	8.0	1400	140050215
2005 Beta 1	Visual Studio 2005 Beta 1 [8.0]	8.0	1400	140040607
—	Windows Server 2003 SP1 DDK (for AMD64)		1400	140040310
2003 SP1	Visual Studio .NET 2003 SP1 [7.1] Visual C++ .NET 2003 SP1 [7.1]	7.1	1310	13106030
—	Windows Server 2003 SP1 DDK		1310	13104035

(continued)

Table A-1   (continued)

Abbreviation	Product	VC++ Version	_MSC_VER	_MSC_FULL_VER
2003	Visual Studio .NET 2003 [7.1] Visual C++ .NET 2003 [7.1]	7.1	1310	13103077
—	Visual Studio Toolkit 2003 [7.1]	7.1	1310	13103052
2003 Beta	Visual Studio .NET 2003 Beta [7.1]	7.1	1310	13102292
—	Windows Server 2003 DDK		1310	13102179
2002	Visual Studio .NET 2002 [7.0] Visual C++ .NET 2002 [7.0]	7.0	1300	13009466
—	Windows XP SP1 DDK		1300	13009176
6.0 SP6	Visual Studio 6.0 SP6 Visual C++ 6.0 SP6	6.0	1200	12008804
6.0 SP5	Visual Studio 6.0 SP5 Visual C++ 6.0 SP5	6.0	1200	12008804
—	Visual Studio 97 [5.0] Visual C++ 5.0	5.0	1100	
—	Visual C++ 4.2	4.2	1020	
—	Visual C++ 4.1	4.1	1010	
—	Visual C++ 4.0	4.0	1000	
—	Visual C++ 2.0	2.0	900	
—	Visual C++ 1.0	1.0	800	
—	Microsoft C/C++ 7.0		700	
—	Microsoft C 6.0		600	

[a]Only IDE has been modified and compiler, The library etc was not changed
[b]Only IDE has been modified and compiler, The library etc was not changed
[c]Since 2017 is binary compatible with 2015, 2017 is not a major upgrade. As a result, the product version and Visual C++ version has been no longer matched
[d]Only IDE has been modified and compiler, The library etc was not changed

- **AdditionalOptions**
  Optional String parameter.
  A list of command-line options. For example, "/<option1> /<option2> /<option#>". Use this parameter to specify command-line options that are not represented by any other task parameter.
  For more information, see Compiler options.

- **AdditionalUsingDirectories**
  Optional String[] parameter.
  Specifies a directory that the compiler will search to resolve file references passed to the **#using** directive.
  For more information, see /AI (specify metadata directories).

- **AlwaysAppend**
  Optional String parameter.
  A string that always gets emitted on the command line. Its default value is "**/c**".

- **AssemblerListingLocation**
  Creates a listing file that contains assembly code.
  For more information, see the **/Fa** option in /FA, /Fa (listing file).

- **AssemblerOutput**
  Optional String parameter.
  Creates a listing file that contains assembly code.
  Specify one of the following values, each of which corresponds to a command-line option:
  o **NoListing**: < *none* >
  o **AssemblyCode**: **/FA**
  o **AssemblyAndMachineCode**: **/FAc**
  o **AssemblyAndSourceCode**: **/FAs**
  o **All**: **/FAcs**
     For more information, see the **/FA**, **/FAc**, **/FAs**, and **/FAcs** options in /FA, /Fa (listing file).

- **BasicRuntimeChecks**
  Optional String parameter.
  Enables and disables the runtime error checks feature, in conjunction with the runtime_checks pragma.
  Specify one of the following values, each of which corresponds to a command-line option:
  o **Default**: < *none* >
  o **StackFrameRuntimeCheck**: **/RTCs**
  o **UninitializedLocalUsageCheck**: **/RTCu**
  o **EnableFastChecks**: **/RTC1**
     For more information, see /RTC (runtime error checks).

- **BrowseInformation**
  Optional Boolean parameter.
  If true, creates a browse information file.
  For more information, see the **/FR** option in /FR, /Fr (create .sbr file).

- **BrowseInformationFile**
  Optional String parameter.
  Specifies a file name for the browse information file.
  For more information, see the **BrowseInformation** parameter in this list, and also see /FR, /Fr (create .sbr file).

- **BufferSecurityCheck**
  Optional Boolean parameter.
  If true, detects some buffer overruns that overwrite the return address, a common technique for exploiting code that does not enforce buffer size restrictions.
  For more information, see /GS (buffer security check).

- **BuildingInIDE**
  Optional Boolean parameter.
  If true, indicates that **MSBuild** is invoked by the IDE. Otherwise, **MSBuild** is invoked on the command line.

- **CallingConvention**
  Optional String parameter.
  Specifies the calling convention, which determines the order in which function arguments are pushed onto the stack, whether the caller function or called function removes the arguments from the stack at the end of the call, and the name-decorating convention that the compiler uses to identify individual functions.
  Specify one of the following values, each of which corresponds to a command-line option:
  o **Cdecl**: **/Gd**
  o **FastCall**: **/Gr**
  o **StdCall**: **/Gz**
     For more information, see /Gd, /Gr, /Gv, /Gz (calling convention).

- **CompileAs**
  Optional String parameter.
  Specifies whether to compile the input file as a C or C++ source file.
  Specify one of the following values, each of which corresponds to a command-line option:
  o **Default**: < *none* >
  o **CompileAsC**: **/TC**
  o **CompileAsCpp**: **/TP**
     For more information, see /Tc, /Tp, /TC, /TP (specify source file type).

- **CompileAsManaged**
  Optional String parameter.
  Enables applications and components to use features from the common language runtime (CLR).
  Specify one of the following values, each of which corresponds to a command-line option:
  o **false**: < *none* >
  o **true**: **/clr**
  o **Pure**: **/clr:pure**
  o **Safe**: **/clr:safe**

   o **OldSyntax**: /clr:oldSyntax

   For more information, see /clr (common language runtime compilation).

- **CreateHotpatchableImage**

  Optional Boolean parameter.

  If true, tells the compiler to prepare an image for *hot patching*. This parameter ensures that the first instruction of each function is two bytes, which is required for hot patching.

  For more information, see /hotpatch (create hotpatchable image).

- **DebugInformationFormat**

  Optional String parameter.

  Selects the type of debugging information created for your program and whether this information is kept in object (*.obj*) files or in a program database (PDB).

  Specify one of the following values, each of which corresponds to a command-line option:

     o **OldStyle**: **/Z7**

     o **ProgramDatabase**: **/Zi**

     o **EditAndContinue**: **/ZI**

     For more information, see /Z7, /Zi, /ZI (debug information format).

- **DisableLanguageExtensions**

  Optional Boolean parameter.

  If **true**, tells the compiler to emit an error for language constructs that are not compatible with either ANSI C or ANSI C++.

  For more information, see the **/Za** option in /Za, /Ze (disable language extensions).

- **DisableSpecificWarnings**

  Optional String[] parameter.

  Disables the warning numbers that are specified in a semicolon-delimited list.

  For more information, see the /wd option in /w, /W0, /W1, /W2, /W3, /W4, /w1, /w2, /w3, /w4, /Wall, /wd, /we, /wo, /Wv, /WX (warning level).

- **EnableEnhancedInstructionSet**

  Optional String parameter.

  Specifies the architecture for code generation that uses the Streaming SIMD Extensions (SSE) and Streaming SIMD Extensions 2 (SSE2) instructions.

  Specify one of the following values, each of which corresponds to a command-line option:

     o **StreamingSIMDExtensions**: **/arch:SSE**

     o **StreamingSIMDExtensions2**: **/arch:SSE2**

     For more information, see /arch (x86).

- **EnableFiberSafeOptimizations**
  Optional Boolean parameter.
  If true, supports fiber safety for data allocated by using static thread-local storage, that is, data allocated by using __declspec(thread).
  For more information, see /GT (support fiber-safe thread-local storage).

- **EnablePREfast**
  Optional Boolean parameter.
  If true, enables code analysis.
  For more information, see /analyze (code analysis).

- **ErrorReporting**
  Optional String parameter.
  Lets you provide internal compiler error (ICE) information directly to Microsoft. By default, the setting in IDE builds is **Prompt**, and the setting in command-line builds is **Queue**.
  Specify one of the following values, each of which corresponds to a command-line option:
  o **None**: **/errorReport:none**
  o **Prompt**: **/errorReport:prompt**
  o **Queue**: **/errorReport:queue**
  o **Send**: **/errorReport:send**
     For more information, see /errorReport (report internal compiler errors).

- **ExceptionHandling**
  Optional String parameter.
  Specifies the model of exception handling to be used by the compiler.
  Specify one of the following values, each of which corresponds to a command-line option:
  o **false**: < *none* >
  o **Async**: **/EHa**
  o **Sync**: **/EHsc**
  o **SyncCThrow**: **/EHs**
     For more information, see /EH (exception handling model).

- **ExpandAttributedSource**
  Optional Boolean parameter.
  If true, creates a listing file that has expanded attributes injected into the source file.
  For more information, see /Fx (merge injected code).

- **FavorSizeOrSpeed**
  Optional String parameter.
  Specifies whether to favor code size or code speed.

Specify one of the following values, each of which corresponds to a command-line option:

o **Neither**: *< none >*
o **Size**: **/Os**
o **Speed**: **/Ot**

For more information, see /Os, /Ot (favor small code, favor fast code).

- **FloatingPointExceptions**
Optional Boolean parameter.
If true, enables the reliable floating-point exception model. Exceptions will be raised immediately after they are triggered.
For more information, see the **/fp:except** option in /fp (specify floating-point behavior).

- **FloatingPointModel**
Optional String parameter.
Sets the floating-point model.
Specify one of the following values, each of which corresponds to a command-line option:

o **Precise**: **/fp:precise**
o **Strict**: **/fp:strict**
o **Fast**: **/fp:fast**

For more information, see /fp (specify floating-point behavior).

- **ForceConformanceInForLoopScope**
Optional Boolean parameter.
If true, implements standard C++ behavior in for loops that use Microsoft extensions (/Ze).
For more information, see /Zc:forScope (force conformance in for loop scope).

- **ForcedIncludeFiles**
Optional **String[]** parameter.
Causes the preprocessor to process one or more specified header files.
For more information, see /FI (name forced include file).

- **ForcedUsingFiles**
Optional **String[]** parameter.
Causes the preprocessor to process one or more specified **#using** files.
For more information, see /FU (name forced #using file).

- **FunctionLevelLinking**
Optional Boolean parameter.
If true, enables the compiler to package individual functions in the form of packaged functions (COMDATs).
For more information, see /Gy (enable function-level linking).

- **GenerateXMLDocumentationFiles**

  Optional Boolean parameter.

  If true, causes the compiler to process documentation comments in source code files and to create an *.xdc* file for each source code file that has documentation comments.

  For more information, see /doc (process documentation comments) (C/C++). Also, see the **XMLDocumentationFileName** parameter in this list.

- **IgnoreStandardIncludePath**

  Optional Boolean parameter.

  If true, prevents the compiler from searching for include files in directories specified in the PATH and INCLUDE environment variables.

  For more information, see /X (ignore standard include paths).

- **InlineFunctionExpansion**

  Optional **String** parameter.

  Specifies the level of inline function expansion for the build.

  Specify one of the following values, each of which corresponds to a command-line option:

  o **Default**: < *none* >
  o **Disabled**: **/Ob0**
  o **OnlyExplicitInline**: **/Ob1**
  o **AnySuitable**: **/Ob2**

     For more information, see /Ob (inline function expansion).

- **IntrinsicFunctions**

  Optional Boolean parameter.

  If true, replaces some function calls with intrinsic or otherwise special forms of the function that help your application run faster.

  For more information, see /Oi (generate intrinsic functions).

- **MinimalRebuild**

  Optional Boolean parameter. This option is deprecated.

  If true, enables minimal rebuild, which determines whether C++ source files that include changed C++ class definitions (stored in header (.h) files) must be recompiled.

  For more information, see /Gm (enable minimal rebuild).

- **MultiProcessorCompilation**

  Optional Boolean parameter.

  If true, uses multiple processors to compile. This parameter creates a process for each effective processor on your computer.

  For more information, see /MP (build with multiple processes). Also, see the **ProcessorNumber** parameter in this list.

- **ObjectFileName**
  Optional **String** parameter.
  Specifies an object (.obj) file name or directory to be used instead of the default.
  For more information, see /Fo (object file name).

- **ObjectFiles**
  Optional **String[]** parameter.
  A list of object files.

- **OmitDefaultLibName**
  Optional Boolean parameter.
  If true, omits the default C runtime library name from the object (*.obj*) file. By
  default, the compiler puts the name of the library into the *.obj* file to direct the
  linker to the correct library.
  For more information, see /Zl (omit default library name).

- **OmitFramePointers**
  Optional Boolean parameter.
  If true, suppresses creation of frame pointers on the call stack.
  For more information, see /Oy (frame-pointer omission).

- **OpenMPSupport**
  Optional Boolean parameter.
  If true, causes the compiler to process OpenMP clauses and directives.
  For more information, see /openmp (enable OpenMP 2.0 support).

- **Optimization**
  Optional **String** parameter.
  Specifies various code optimizations for speed and size.
  Specify one of the following values, each of which corresponds to a command-
  line option:
  - **Disabled**: **/Od**
  - **MinSpace**: **/O1**
  - **MaxSpeed**: **/O2**
  - **Full**: **/Ox**
    For more information, see /O options (optimize code).

- **PrecompiledHeader**
  Optional **String** parameter.
  Create or use a precompiled header (*.pch*) file during the build.
  Specify one of the following values, each of which corresponds to a command-
  line option:
  - **NotUsing**: < *none* >
  - **Create**: **/Yc**
  - **Use**: **/Yu**

For more information, see /Yc (create precompiled header file) and /Yu (use precompiled header file). Also, see the **PrecompiledHeaderFile** and **PrecompiledHeaderOutputFile** parameters in this list.

- **PrecompiledHeaderFile**
  Optional **String** parameter.
  Specifies a precompiled header file name to create or use.
  For more information, see /Yc (create precompiled header file) and /Yu (use precompiled header file).

- **PrecompiledHeaderOutputFile**
  Optional **String** parameter.
  Specifies a path name for a precompiled header instead of using the default path name.
  For more information, see /Fp (name .pch file).

- **PreprocessKeepComments**
  Optional Boolean parameter.
  If true, preserves comments during preprocessing.
  For more information, see /C (preserve comments during preprocessing).

- **PreprocessorDefinitions**
  Optional String[] parameter.
  Defines a preprocessing symbol for your source file.
  For more information, see /D (preprocessor definitions).

- **PreprocessOutput**
  Optional ITaskItem[] parameter.
  Defines an array of preprocessor output items that can be consumed and emitted by tasks.

- **PreprocessOutputPath**
  Optional String parameter.
  Specifies the name of the output file to which the **PreprocessToFile** parameter writes preprocessed output.
  For more information, see /Fi (preprocess output file name).

- **PreprocessSuppressLineNumbers**
  Optional Boolean parameter.
  If true, preprocesses C and C++ source files and copies the preprocessed files to the standard output device.
  For more information, see /EP (preprocess to stdout without #line directives).

- **PreprocessToFile**
  Optional Boolean parameter.
  If true, preprocesses C and C++ source files and writes the preprocessed output to a file.
  For more information, see /P (preprocess to a file).

- **ProcessorNumber**
  Optional Integer parameter.
  Specifies the maximum number of processors to use in a multiprocessor compilation. Use this parameter in combination with the **MultiProcessorCompilation** parameter.

- **ProgramDataBaseFileName**
  Optional String parameter.
  Specifies a file name for the program database (PDB) file.
  For more information, see /Fd (program database file name).

- **RuntimeLibrary**
  Optional String parameter.
  Indicates whether a multithreaded module is a DLL and selects retail or debug versions of the runtime library.
  Specify one of the following values, each of which corresponds to a command-line option:
  - **MultiThreaded**: **/MT**
  - **MultiThreadedDebug**: **/MTd**
  - **MultiThreadedDLL**: **/MD**
  - **MultiThreadedDebugDLL**: **/MDd**
    For more information, see /MD, /MT, /LD (use runtime library).

- **RuntimeTypeInfo**
  Optional Boolean parameter.
  If true, adds code to check C++ object types at runtime (runtime type information).
  For more information, see /GR (enable runtime type information).

- **ShowIncludes**
  Optional Boolean parameter.
  If true, causes the compiler to output a list of the include files.
  For more information, see /showIncludes (list include files).

- **SmallerTypeCheck**
  Optional Boolean parameter.
  If true, reports a runtime error if a value is assigned to a smaller data type and causes a data loss.
  For more information, see the **/RTCc** option in /RTC (runtime error checks).

- **Sources**
  Required ITaskItem[] parameter.
  Specifies a list of source files separated by spaces.

- **StringPooling**
  Optional Boolean parameter.
  If true, enables the compiler to create one copy of identical strings in the program image.
  For more information, see /GF (eliminate duplicate strings).

- **StructMemberAlignment**
  Optional String parameter.
  Specifies the byte alignment for all members in a structure.
  Specify one of the following values, each of which corresponds to a command-line option:
  - **Default**: **/Zp1**
  - **1Byte**: **/Zp1**
  - **2Bytes**: **/Zp2**
  - **4Bytes**: **/Zp4**
  - **8Bytes**: **/Zp8**
  - **16Bytes**: **/Zp16**
    For more information, see /Zp (struct member alignment).

- **SuppressStartupBanner**
  Optional Boolean parameter.
  If true, prevents the display of the copyright and version number message when the task starts.
  For more information, see /nologo (suppress startup banner) (C/C++).

- **TrackerLogDirectory**
  Optional String parameter.
  Specifies the intermediate directory where tracking logs for this task are stored.
  For more information, see the **TLogReadFiles** and **TLogWriteFiles** parameters in this list.

- **TreatSpecificWarningsAsErrors**
  Optional **String[]** parameter.
  Treats the specified list of compiler warnings as errors.
  For more information, see the **/wen** option in /w, /W0, /W1, /W2, /W3, /W4, /w1, /w2, /w3, /w4, /Wall, /wd, /we, /wo, /Wv, /WX (warning level).

- **TreatWarningAsError**
  Optional Boolean parameter.
  If true, treats all compiler warnings as errors.

For more information, see the **/WX** option in /w, /W0, /W1, /W2, /W3, /W4, /w1, /w2, /w3, /w4, /Wall, /wd, /we, /wo, /Wv, /WX (warning level).

- **TreatWChar_tAsBuiltInType**
  Optional Boolean parameter.
  If true, treats the wchar_t type as a native type.
  For more information, see /Zc:wchar_t (wchar_t is a native type).

- **UndefineAllPreprocessorDefinitions**
  Optional Boolean parameter.
  If true, undefines the Microsoft-specific symbols that the compiler defines.
  For more information, see the **/u** option in /U, /u (undefine symbols).

- **UndefinePreprocessorDefinitions**
  Optional String[] parameter.
  Specifies a list of one or more preprocessor symbols to undefine.
  For more information, see the **/U** option in /U, /u (undefine symbols).

- **UseFullPaths**
  Optional Boolean parameter.
  If true, displays the full path of source code files passed to the compiler in diagnostics.
  For more information, see /FC (full path of source code file in diagnostics).

- **UseUnicodeForAssemblerListing**
  Optional Boolean parameter.
  If true, causes the output file to be created in UTF-8 format.
  For more information, see the **/FAu** option in /FA, /Fa (listing file).

- **WarningLevel**
  Optional String parameter.
  Specifies the highest level of warning that is to be generated by the compiler.
  Specify one of the following values, each of which corresponds to a command-line option:
  - **TurnOffAllWarnings**: **/W0**
  - **Level1**: **/W1**
  - **Level2**: **/W2**
  - **Level3**: **/W3**
  - **Level4**: **/W4**
  - **EnableAllWarnings**: **/Wall**
    For more information, see the **/W**n option in /w, /W0, /W1, /W2, /W3, /W4, /w1, /w2, /w3, /w4, /Wall, /wd, /we, /wo, /Wv, /WX (warning level).

- **WholeProgramOptimization**
  Optional Boolean parameter.
  If true, enables whole program optimization.
  For more information, see /GL (whole program optimization).

- **XMLDocumentationFileName**
  Optional String parameter.
  Specifies the name of the generated XML documentation files. This parameter can be a file or directory name.
  For more information, see the name argument in /doc (process documentation comments) (C/C++). Also, see the **GenerateXMLDocumentationFiles** parameter in this list.

- **MinimalRebuildFromTracking**
  Optional Boolean parameter.
  If true, a tracked incremental build is performed; if false, a rebuild is performed.

- **TLogReadFiles**
  Optional ITaskItem[] parameter.
  Specifies an array of items that represent the *read file tracking logs*.
  A read file tracking log (*.tlog*) contains the names of the input files that are read by a task and is used by the project build system to support incremental builds. For more information, see the **TrackerLogDirectory** and **TrackFileAccess** parameters in this list.

- **TLogWriteFiles**
  Optional ITaskItem[] parameter.
  Specifies an array of items that represent the *write file tracking logs*.
  A write file tracking log (*.tlog*) contains the names of the output files that are written by a task and is used by the project build system to support incremental builds. For more information, see the **TrackerLogDirectory** and **TrackFileAccess** parameters in this list.

- **TrackFileAccess**
  Optional Boolean parameter.
  If true, tracks file access patterns.
  For more information, see the **TLogReadFiles** and **TLogWriteFiles** parameters in this list.

Microsoft C/C++ Compiler Options Listed by Category

The material in this section is based on data from the site [12].

This section contains a categorical list of compiler options. For an alphabetical list, see Compiler Options Listed Alphabetically from the site [12].

Optimization

Table A-2 Microsoft C/C++ compiler options: Optimization

Option	Purpose
/favor:<blend|AMD64|INTEL64|ATOM>	Produces code that is optimized for a specified architecture or for a range of architectures.
/O1	Creates small code.
/O2	Creates fast code.
/Ob<n>	Controls inline expansion.
/Od	Disables optimization.
/Og	Deprecated. Uses global optimizations.
/Oi[-]	Generates intrinsic functions.
/Os	Favors small code.
/Ot	Favors fast code.
/Ox	A subset of /O2 that doesn't include /GF or /Gy.
/Oy	Omits frame pointer (x86 only).

Code Generation

Table A-3 Microsoft C/C++ compiler options: Code generation

Option	Purpose
/arch:<IA32|SSE|SSE2|AVX|AVX2|AVX512>	Minimum CPU architecture requirements. IA32, SSE, and SSE2 are x86 only.
/clr	Produces an output file to run on the common language runtime.
/clr:implicitKeepAlive-	Turns off implicit emission of System::GC::KeepAlive(this).
/clr:initialAppDomain	Enables initial AppDomain behavior of Visual C++ 2002.
/clr:netcore	Produces assemblies targeting .NET Core runtime.
/clr:noAssembly	Doesn't produce an assembly.
/clr:nostdimport	Doesn't import any required assemblies implicitly.

(continued)

Table A-3 (continued)

Option	Purpose
/clr:nostdlib	Ignores the system .NET framework directory when searching for assemblies.
/clr:pure	Produces an IL-only output file (no native executable code).
/clr:safe	Produces an IL-only verifiable output file.
/EHa	Enables C++ exception handling (with SEH exceptions).
/EHc	extern "C" defaults to nothrow.
/EHr	Always generates noexcept runtime termination checks.
/EHs	Enables C++ exception handling (no SEH exceptions).
/fp:contract	Considers floating-point contractions when generating code.
/fp:except[-]	Considers floating-point exceptions when generating code.
/fp:fast	"fast" floating-point model; results are less predictable.
/fp:precise	"precise" floating-point model; results are predictable.
/fp:strict	"strict" floating-point model (implies /fp:except).
/fpcvt:BC	Backward-compatible floating-point to unsigned integer conversions.
/fpcvt:IA	Intel native floating-point to unsigned integer conversion behavior.
/fsanitize	Enables compilation of sanitizer instrumentation such as AddressSanitizer.
/fsanitize-coverage	Enables compilation of code coverage instrumentation for libraries such as LibFuzzer.
/GA	Optimizes for Windows applications.
/Gd	Uses the __cdecl calling convention (x86 only).
/Ge	Deprecated. Activates stack probes.
/GF	Enables string pooling.
/Gh	Calls hook function _penter.
/GH	Calls hook function _pexit.
/GL[-]	Enables whole program optimization.
/Gm[-]	Deprecated. Enables minimal rebuild.
/Gr	Uses the __fastcall calling convention (x86 only).
/GR[-]	Enables runtime type information (RTTI).
/GS[-]	Checks buffer security.

(continued)

Table A-3 (continued)

Option	Purpose
/Gs[n]	Controls stack probes.
/GT	Supports fiber safety for data allocated by using static thread-local storage.
/Gu[-]	Ensures distinct functions have distinct addresses.
/guard:cf[-]	Adds control flow guard security checks.
/guard:ehcont[-]	Enables EH continuation metadata.
/Gv	Uses the __**vectorcall** calling convention (x86 and x64 only).
/Gw[-]	Enables whole-program global data optimization.
/GX[-]	Deprecated. Enables synchronous exception handling. Use /EH instead.
/Gy[-]	Enables function-level linking.
/Gz	Uses the __**stdcall** calling convention (x86 only).
/GZ	Deprecated. Enables fast checks (same as /RTC1).
/homeparams	Forces parameters passed in registers to be written to their locations on the stack upon function entry. This compiler option is only for the x64 compilers (native and cross compile).
/hotpatch	Creates a hotpatchable image.
/Qfast_transcendentals	Generates fast transcendentals.
/QIfist	Deprecated. Suppresses the call of the helper function _ftol when a conversion from a floating-point type to an integral type is required (x86 only).
/Qimprecise_fwaits	Removes fwait commands inside **try** blocks.
/QIntel-jcc-erratum	Mitigates the performance impact of the Intel JCC erratum microcode update.
/Qpar	Enables automatic parallelization of loops.
/Qpar-report:n	Enables reporting levels for automatic parallelization.
/Qsafe_fp_loads	Uses integer move instructions for floating-point values and disables certain floating-point load optimizations.
/Qspectre[-]	Enables mitigations for CVE 2017-5753, for a class of Spectre attacks.
/Qspectre-load	Generates serializing instructions for every load instruction.
/Qspectre-load-cf	Generates serializing instructions for every control flow instruction that loads memory.

(continued)

Table A-3 (continued)

Option	Purpose
/Qvec-report:n	Enables reporting levels for automatic vectorization.
/RTC1	Enables fast runtime checks (equivalent to /RTCsu).
/RTCc	Converts to smaller type checks at runtime.
/RTCs	Enables stack frame runtime checks.
/RTCu	Enables uninitialized local usage checks.
/volatile:iso	Acquires/releases semantics not guaranteed on volatile accesses.
/volatile:ms	Acquires/releases semantics guaranteed on volatile accesses.

Output Files

Table A-4 Microsoft C/C++ compiler options: Output files

Option	Purpose
/doc	Processes documentation comments to an XML file.
/FA	Configures an assembly listing file.
/Fa	Creates an assembly listing file.
/Fd	Renames the program database file.
/Fe	Renames the executable file.
/Fi	Specifies the preprocessed output file name.
/Fm	Creates a mapfile.
/Fo	Creates an object file.
/Fp	Specifies a precompiled header file name.
/FR, /Fr	Name generated *.sbr* browser files. **/Fr** is deprecated.
/Ft<dir>	Location of the header files generated for #import.

Preprocessor

Table A-5 Microsoft C/C++ compiler options: Preprocessor

Option	Purpose
/AI<dir>	Specifies a directory to search to resolve file references passed to the #using directive.
/C	Preserves comments during preprocessing.
/D<name>{=|#}<text>	Defines constants and macros.
/E	Copies preprocessor output to standard output.
/EP	Copies preprocessor output to standard output.
/FI<file>	Preprocesses the specified include file.
/FU<file>	Forces the use of a file name, as if it had been passed to the #using directive.
/Fx	Merges injected code with the source file.
/I<dir>	Searches a directory for include files.
/P	Writes preprocessor output to a file.
/PD	Prints all macro definitions.
/PH	Generates #pragma file_hash when preprocessing.
/U<name>	Removes a predefined macro.
/u	Removes all predefined macros.
/X	Ignores the standard include directory.

Header Units/Modules

Table A-6 Microsoft C/C++ compiler options: Header units/modules

Option	Purpose
/exportHeader	Creates the header unit files (.*ifc*) specified by the input arguments.
/headerUnit	Specifies where to find the header unit file (.*ifc*) for the specified header.
/headerName	Builds a header unit from the specified header.
/ifcOutput	Specifies the output file name or directory for built .*ifc* files.
/interface	Treats the input file as a module interface unit.
/internalPartition	Treats the input file as an internal partition unit.
/reference	Uses named module IFC.
/scanDependencies	Lists module and header unit dependencies in C++ Standard JSON form.
/sourceDependencies	Lists all source-level dependencies.
/sourceDependencies:directives	Lists module and header unit dependencies.
/translateInclude	Treats #include as import.

Language

Table A-7   Microsoft C/C++ compiler options: Language

Option	Purpose
/await	Enables coroutine (resumable function) extensions.
/await:strict	Enables standard C++20 coroutine support with earlier language versions.
/constexpr:backtrace\<N>	Shows N constexpr evaluations in diagnostics (default: 10).
/constexpr:depth\<N>	Recursion depth limit for constexpr evaluation (default: 512).
/constexpr:steps\<N>	Terminates constexpr evaluation after N steps (default: 100000)
/openmp	Enables #pragma omp in source code.
/openmp:experimental	Enables OpenMP 2.0 language extensions plus select OpenMP 3.0+ language extensions.
/openmp:llvm	OpenMP language extensions using LLVM runtime.
/permissive[-]	Sets the standard-conformance mode.
/std:c++14	C++14 standard ISO/IEC 14882:2014 (default).
/std:c++17	C++17 standard ISO/IEC 14882:2017.
/std:c++20	C++20 standard ISO/IEC 14882:2020.
/std:c++latest	The latest draft C++ standard preview features.
/std:c11	C11 standard ISO/IEC 9899:2011.
/std:c17	C17 standard ISO/IEC 9899:2018.
/vd{0|1|2}	Suppresses or enables hidden vtordisp class members.
/vmb	Uses the best base for pointers to members.
/vmg	Uses full generality for pointers to members.
/vmm	Declares multiple inheritance.
/vms	Declares single inheritance.
/vmv	Declares virtual inheritance.
/Z7	Generates C 7.0–compatible debugging information.
/Za	Disables some C89 language extensions in C code.
/Zc:__cplusplus[-]	Enables the __cplusplus macro to report the supported standard (off by default).
/Zc:__STDC__	Enables the __STDC__ macro to report the C standard is supported (off by default).
/Zc:alignedNew[-]	Enables C++17 over-aligned dynamic allocation (on by default in C++17).
/Zc:auto[-]	Enforces the new Standard C++ meaning for **auto** (on by default).
/Zc:char8_t[-]	Enables or disables C++20 native u8 literal support as const char8_t (off by default, except under **/std:c++20**).
/Zc:enumTypes[-]	Enables Standard C++ rules for inferred enum base types (off by default, not implied by **/permissive-**).

(continued)

Table A-7   (continued)

Option	Purpose
/Zc:externC[-]	Enforces Standard C++ rules for extern "C" functions (implied by **/permissive-**).
/Zc:externConstexpr[-]	Enables external linkage for **constexpr** variables (off by default).
/Zc:forScope[-]	Enforces Standard C++ **for** scoping rules (on by default).
/Zc:gotoScope	Enforces Standard C++ **goto** rules around local variable initialization (implied by **/permissive-**).
/Zc:hiddenFriend[-]	Enforces Standard C++ hidden friend rules (implied by **/permissive-**).
/Zc:implicitNoexcept[-]	Enables implicit **noexcept** on required functions (on by default).
/Zc:inline[-]	Removes unreferenced functions or data if they're COMDAT or have internal linkage only (off by default).
/Zc:lambda[-]	Enables new lambda processor for conformance-mode syntactic checks in generic lambdas.
/Zc:noexceptTypes[-]	Enforces C++17 **noexcept** rules (on by default in C++17 or later).
/Zc:nrvo[-]	Enables optional copy and move elisions (on by default under **/O2**, **/permissive-**, or **/std:c++20** or later).
/Zc:preprocessor[-]	Uses the new conforming preprocessor (off by default, except in C11/C17).
/Zc:referenceBinding[-]	A UDT temporary won't bind to a non-const lvalue reference (off by default).
/Zc:rvalueCast[-]	Enforces Standard C++ explicit type conversion rules (off by default).
/Zc:sizedDealloc[-]	Enables C++14 global sized deallocation functions (on by default).
/Zc:strictStrings[-]	Disables string literal to char* or wchar_t* conversion (off by default).
/Zc:templateScope[-]	Enforces Standard C++ template parameter shadowing rules (off by default).
/Zc:ternary[-]	Enforces conditional operator rules on operand types (off by default).
/Zc:threadSafeInit[-]	Enables thread-safe local static initialization (on by default).
/Zc:throwingNew[-]	Assumes **operator new** throws on failure (off by default).
/Zc:tlsGuards[-]	Generates runtime checks for TLS variable initialization (on by default).
/Zc:trigraphs	Enables trigraphs (obsolete, off by default).
/Zc:twoPhase[-]	Uses nonconforming template parsing behavior (conforming by default).
/Zc:wchar_t[-]	**wchar_t** is a native type, not a typedef (on by default).
/Zc:zeroSizeArrayNew[-]	Calls member new/delete for 0-size arrays of objects (on by default).

(continued)

Table A-7 (continued)

Option	Purpose
/Ze	Deprecated. Enables C89 language extensions.
/Zf	Improves PDB generation time in parallel builds.
/ZH:[MD5|SHA1|SHA_256]	Specifies MD5, SHA-1, or SHA-256 for checksums in debug info.
/ZI	Includes debug information in a program database compatible with Edit and Continue (x86 only).
/Zi	Generates complete debugging information.
/Zl	Removes the default library name from the *.obj* file.
/Zo[-]	Generates richer debugging information for optimized code.
/Zp[n]	Packs structure members.
/Zs	Checks syntax only.
/ZW	Produces an output file to run on the Windows Runtime.

Linking

Table A-8 Microsoft C/C++ compiler options: Linking

Option	Purpose
/F	Sets stack size.
/LD	Creates a dynamic-link library.
/LDd	Creates a debug dynamic-link library.
/link	Passes the specified option to LINK.
/LN	Creates an MSIL .netmodule.
/MD	Compiles to create a multithreaded DLL, by using *MSVCRT.lib*.
/MDd	Compiles to create a debug multithreaded DLL, by using *MSVCRTD.lib*.
/MT	Compiles to create a multithreaded executable file, by using *LIBCMT.lib*.
/MTd	Compiles to create a debug multithreaded executable file, by using *LIBCMTD.lib*.

Miscellaneous

Table A-9 Microsoft C/C++ compiler options: Miscellaneous

Option	Purpose
/?	Lists the compiler options.
@	Specifies a response file.
/analyze	Enables code analysis.
/bigobj	Increases the number of addressable sections in an .obj file.
/c	Compiles without linking.
/cgthreads	Specifies the number of *cl.exe* threads to use for optimization and code generation.
/errorReport	Deprecated. Error reporting is controlled by Windows Error Reporting (WER) settings.
/execution-charset	Sets the execution character set.
/fastfail	Enables fast-fail mode.
/FC	Displays the full path of source code files passed to *cl.exe* in diagnostic text.
/FS	Forces writes to the PDB file to be serialized through *MSPDBSRV.EXE*.
/H	Deprecated. Restricts the length of external (public) names.
/HELP	Lists the compiler options.
/J	Changes the default **char** type.
/JMC	Supports native C++ Just My Code debugging.
/kernel	The compiler and linker will create a binary that can be executed in the Windows kernel.
/MP	Builds multiple source files concurrently.
/nologo	Suppresses display of sign-on banner.
/presetPadding	Zero-initializes padding for stack-based class types.
/showIncludes	Displays a list of all include files during compilation.
/source-charset	Sets the source character set.
/Tc	Specifies a C source file.
/TC	Specifies all source files are C.
/Tp	Specifies a C++ source file.
/TP	Specifies all source files are C++.
/utf-8	Sets source and execution character sets to UTF-8.
/V	Deprecated. Sets the version string.
/validate-charset	Validates UTF-8 files for only compatible characters.
/volatileMetadata	Generates metadata on volatile memory accesses.
/Yc	Creates a *.PCH* file.
/Yd	Deprecated. Places complete debugging information in all object files. Use /Zi instead.
/Yl	Injects a PCH reference when creating a debug library.
/Yu	Uses a precompiled header file during build.
/Y-	Ignores all other precompiled header compiler options in the current build.
/Zm	Specifies the precompiled header memory allocation limit.

Diagnostics

Table A-10 Microsoft C/C++ compiler options: Diagnostics

Option	Purpose
/diagnostics:caret[-]	Diagnostics format: prints column and the indicated line of source.
/diagnostics:classic	Uses legacy diagnostics format.
/diagnostics	Diagnostics format: prints column information.
/external:anglebrackets	Treats all headers included via < > as external.
/external:env:<var>	Specifies an environment variable with locations of external headers.
/external:I <path>	Specifies location of external headers.
/external:templates[-]	Evaluates warning level across template instantiation chain.
/external:W<n>	Sets the warning level for external headers.
/options:strict	Unrecognized compiler options are errors.
/sdl	Enables more security features and warnings.
/w	Disables all warnings.
/W0, /W1, /W2, /W3, /W4	Sets the output warning level.
/w1<n>, /w2<n>, /w3<n>, /w4<n>	Sets the warning level for the specified warning.
/Wall	Enables all warnings, including warnings that are disabled by default.
/wd<n>	Disables the specified warning.
/we<n>	Treats the specified warning as an error.
/WL	Enables one-line diagnostics for error and warning messages when compiling C++ source code from the command line.
/wo<n>	Displays the specified warning only once.
/Wv:xx[.yy[.zzzzz]]	Disables warnings introduced after the specified version of the compiler.
/WX	Treats warnings as errors.

Experimental Options

Experimental options may only be supported by certain versions of the compiler. They may also behave differently in different compiler versions. Often the best, or only, documentation for experimental options is in the Microsoft C++ Team Blog.

Table A-11 Microsoft C/C++ compiler options: Experimental options

Option	Purpose
/experimental:module	Enables experimental module support.

Deprecated and Removed Compiler Options

Table A-12 Microsoft C/C++ compiler options: Deprecated and removed compiler options

Option	Purpose
/clr:noAssembly	Deprecated. Use /LN (Create MSIL Module) instead.
/errorReport	Deprecated. Error reporting is controlled by Windows Error Reporting (WER) settings.
/experimental:preprocessor	Deprecated. Enables experimental conforming preprocessor support. Use /Zc:preprocessor
/Fr	Deprecated. Creates a browse information file without local variables.
/Ge	Deprecated. Activates stack probes. On by default.
/Gm	Deprecated. Enables minimal rebuild.
/GX	Deprecated. Enables synchronous exception handling. Use /EH instead.
/GZ	Deprecated. Enables fast checks. Use /RTC1 instead.
/H	Deprecated. Restricts the length of external (public) names.
/Og	Deprecated. Uses global optimizations.
/QIfist	Deprecated. Once used to specify how to convert from a floating-point type to an integral type.
/V	Deprecated. Sets the *.obj* file version string.
/Wp64	Obsolete. Detects 64-bit portability problems.
/Yd	Deprecated. Places complete debugging information in all object files. Use /Zi instead.
/Zc:forScope-	Deprecated. Disables conformance in for loop scope.
/Ze	Deprecated. Enables language extensions.
/Zg	Removed in Visual Studio 2015. Generates function prototypes.

Bibliography

[1] American National Standard INCITS-ISO-IEC 9899-2011. 2012. *Information technology: Programming languages – C*, 702. ANSI. May 23.

[2] International Standard ISO-IEC 14882-2014. 2014. *Information technology: Programming languages – C++*, 4th ed., 1358. ISO Office. December 15.

[3] Albahari, Joseph, and Ben Albahari. 2012. *C# 5.0 in a Nutshell*, 5th ed. O'Reilly.

[4] Scheinerman, Edward. 2006. *C++ for Mathematicians. An Introduction for Students and Professionals*, 521. Chapman & Hall-CRC.

[5] Press, William H., Saul A. Teukolsky, William T. Vetterling, and Brian P. Flannery. 2007. *Numerical Recipes. The Art of Scientific Computing*, 3rd ed., 1235. Cambridge University Press.

[6] Barone, Luciano Maria et al. 2013. *Scientific Programming: C-Language, Algorithms and Models in Science*, 718. World Scientific.

[7] Garrido, Jose M. 2013. *Introduction to Computational Modeling Using C and Open-Source Tools*, 461. Chapman & Hall-CRC.

[8] Solomon, Justin. 2015. *Numerical Algorithms: Methods for Computer Vision, Machine Learning, and Graphics*, 400. CRC Press.

[9] Kneusel, Ronald T. 2015. *Numbers and Computers*, 231. Springer.

[10] Yan, Song Y. 2013. *Computational Number Theory and Modern Cryptography*, 425. Wiley.

[11] CL task. Available online: https://learn.microsoft.com/en-us/visualstudio/msbuild/cl-task?view=vs-2022

[12] Compiler Options. Available online: https://learn.microsoft.com/en-us/cpp/build/reference/compiler-options?view=msvc-170

[13] Walkthrough: Using MSBuild to Create a Visual C++ Project. Available online: https://learn.microsoft.com/en-us/cpp/build/walkthrough-using-msbuild-to-create-a-visual-cpp-project?redirectedfrom=MSDN&view=msvc-170

[14] Visual Studio 2019 System Requirements. Available online: https://docs.microsoft.com/en-us/visualstudio/releases/2019/system-requirements

[15] Visual Studio 2022 Product Family System Requirements. Available online: https://docs.microsoft.com/en-us/visualstudio/releases/2022/system-requirements

[16] Download the Windows Driver Kit (WDK). Available online: https://docs.microsoft.com/en-us/windows-hardware/drivers/download-the-wdk

[17] Microsoft Enterprise WDK License for VS 2015. Available online: https://docs.microsoft.com/en-us/legal/windows/hardware/enterprise-wdk-license-2015

[18] Microsoft Enterprise WDK License for VS 2017. Available online: https://docs.microsoft.com/en-us/legal/windows/hardware/enterprise-wdk-license-2017

[19] Microsoft Enterprise WDK License for VS 2019. Available online: https://docs.microsoft.com/en-us/legal/windows/hardware/enterprise-wdk-license-2019

© The Author(s), under exclusive license to APress Media, LLC,
part of Springer Nature 2024
B. I. Tuleuov, A. B. Ospanova, *Beginning C++ Compilers*,
https://doi.org/10.1007/978-1-4842-9563-2

[20] Microsoft Enterprise WDK License for VS 2019. Available online: https://docs.microsoft.com/en-us/legal/windows/hardware/enterprise-wdk-license-2019-New

[21] Microsoft Enterprise WDK License for VS 2022. Available online: https://docs.microsoft.com/en-us/legal/windows/hardware/enterprise-wdk-license-2022

[22] Using the Enterprise WDK. Available online: https://docs.microsoft.com/en-us/windows-hardware/drivers/develop/using-the-enterprise-wdk

[23] MSBuild response files. Available online: https://learn.microsoft.com/en-us/visualstudio/msbuild/msbuild-response-files?view=vs-2022

[24] Griffith, Arthur. *GCC: The Complete Reference*. McGraw-Hill, 2002.

[25] Walkthrough: Create and use a static library. Available online: https://learn.microsoft.com/en-us/cpp/build/walkthrough-creating-and-using-a-static-library-cpp?view=msvc-170

[26] Walkthrough: Create and use your own Dynamic Link Library (C++). Available online: https://learn.microsoft.com/en-us/cpp/build/walkthrough-creating-and-using-a-dynamic-link-library-cpp?view=msvc-170

[27] Universal CRT deployment. Available online: https://learn.microsoft.com/en-us/cpp/windows/universal-crt-deployment?view=msvc-170

[28] Configuring programs for Windows XP. Available online: https://learn.microsoft.com/en-us/cpp/build/configuring-programs-for-windows-xp?view=msvc-170

[29] List of _MSC_VER and _MSC_FULL_VER. Available online: https://dev.to/yumetodo/list-of-mscver-and-mscfullver-8nd

[30] Hyde, Randall. 2022. *The Art of 64-Bit Assembly*. Volume 1, x86-64 Machine Organization and Programming, 1001. San Francisco: No Starch Press Inc.

[31] GNU MP Manual. Available online: http://gmplib.org/manual/, http://gmplib.org/gmp-man-6.0.0a.pdf

[32] MPFR Reference Manual. Available online: www.mpfr.org/mpfr-current/mpfr.html, www.mpfr.org/mpfr-current/mpfr.pdf

Index

© The Author(s), under exclusive license to APress Media, LLC,
part of Springer Nature 2024
B. I. Tuleuov, A. B. Ospanova, *Beginning C++ Compilers*,
https://doi.org/10.1007/978-1-4842-9563-2

Printed in the United States
by Baker & Taylor Publisher Services